To the bride of Christ,

broken and beloved.

CONTENTS

INTRODUCTION

STILL EVANGELICAL?

MARK LABBERTON

E vangelicalism in America has cracked, split on the shoals of the 2016 presidential election and its aftermath, leaving many wondering whether they want to be in or out of the evangelical tribe. For a movement with a high public profile and much influence in American religion, culture, and politics—perhaps providing determinative support for the election of Donald Trump—it matters when that influence itself is breaking up the evangelical camp.

Contentiousness brought to the fore by the election surrounds what it means to affirm and demonstrate evangelical Christian faith amid the messy and polarized realities gripping our country and world. Desperation, anger, pain, frustration, and fear are evident on nearly every horizon. Within the relatively broad evangelical family, the election made apparent that culture rivals the gospel in defining evangelical political vision; our sociological frame speaks louder than our theology. This is not new to American evangelicalism (nor mainline Protestantism), but it is now more blatant and more critical. For a movement that has been about the primacy of Christian faith, this is a crisis.

This collection of essays offers perspectives and reflections from a spectrum of people who could be seen as insiders to the evangelical movement. The book isn't trying to advance a single perspective or to speak for evangelicalism at large. For some, the story is about a historical movement; for others, it's more about their own story. All the writers speak for themselves as they wrestle with and offer their response to "Still evangelical?" in light of their convictions. All of these writers are more than aware that the word *evangelical* is understandably being declared dead and buried by some voices who find the word hopelessly entrapped in a particular and problematic political vision. This means contributors to this volume probably have varying attitudes about whether the term *evangelical* or *evangelicalism* has any meaningful viability or necessity, and the associations it accrues daily may make that more difficult to sustain. All of these writers, however, would maintain the distinct importance of the evangel that lies at the heart of our faith and life.

"Still evangelical?" is a question at the intersection of Christian faith and public life, but its urgency and pathos do not have to do primarily with evangelicalism as a movement. Rather, they have to do with how this part of the Christian family defines its central mission: to follow Jesus Christ and to love our neighbors and enemies in word and act, especially in troubled and conflicted times. What matters most, therefore, is the *evangel*—the *good news*—not evangelicalism. But for many, it's the evangel that current evangelicalism seems to put at risk.

A THEOLOGICAL IDENTITY AND
A THEO-POLITICAL BRAND

The 2016 election may have been the occasion for this drama, but it isn't the cause. For starters, it needs to be said that the battle afoot has little to do with theology proper. In part, this reveals that the word *evangelical* has morphed in common usage from being a reference to a set of primary theological commitments into something akin to a passionately defended, theo-political brand. The word *evangelical* has become a kind of litmus test with which certain gatekeepers draw interpretive lines. Crossing those lines can mean paying a steep and intractable price in the name of theology, but tends to be more about sociology and ideology. Alternatively, to stay within those lines is anathema to people who, because of their faith and social location, find the sectarian biases of white evangelicals especially to be more and more like religiously justified social bigotry and therefore an unsustainable context for their lives and especially for their faith in the good news.

In its current mode, evangelicalism contains an amalgam of theological views, partisan political debates, regional power blocks, populist visions, racial biases, and cultural anxieties, all mixed in an ethos of fear. No wonder it can be difficult to know whether one is still evangelical. The impression of many on the evangelical left is that the good news of Jesus Christ has been taken hostage by a highly charged, toxic subculture on the evangelical right that—in the name of God—expresses steely resolve to have its own way in the public square. From the evangelical right, the critique is that Christian America is at war with any and all liberalism—evangelical or otherwise—and is in serious danger of losing its conservative virtues and spiritual practices. The Bible may be quoted in various ways, but arguments on all sides often seem more ideological than biblical.

After the fundamentalist-modernist controversy of the 1920s, the more conservative end of the American Protestant movement eventually divided along theological and cultural lines. Fundamentalists continued to defend a tight, originalist orientation in their understanding of the Bible, its inerrant authority, and its implications for social relations, not least for the role of women in leadership. Fundamentalism tends to see itself as a bastion of faithfulness defending the faith against secular opponents and Christian compromisers (evangelicals and liberals both).

In contrast to this is the rise of a more distinct evangelicalism that maintains Christian orthodoxy but does so with a greater engagement with and receptivity to culture and to critical self-reflection. This history has led to the two branches of what today is called evangelicalism. While sharing many theological commitments, they have very different social locations and hold very different mental frames for the values they affirm.

Fundamentalism's attraction to theological and social purity plays easily into a theologized ideology that fits what many think of as the religious right. As a movement refined in earlier battles in the first quarter of the twentieth century, the social birthright of fundamentalism can still be very much on display. Evangelicalism's greater receptivity and engagement with culture and diversity has never mixed easily or happily with the more boundary-keeping fundamentalism.

Today's press represents this spectrum as one movement, which it calls evangelicalism. In the media coverage of conservative Christianity, somewhere along the line the distinction between fundamentalists and evangelicals was lost, and the two were conflated. Perhaps this has much to do with an inclination of both groups to position themselves in the middle, with delineations given up in favor of a broader commonality. The consequence is that a large block can be designated "evangelical," but this is so broad it fails to delineate basic differences. In the end, a lot of what has been dubbed evangelical in recent media coverage probably more aptly fits fundamentalism.

However, is all this just in-house debate? The more compelling issue is not whether evangelicals should be cast with fundamentalists but whether Christian witness is evangel-centric in character, motive, expression, and integrity. Is the evangel defining and shaping evangelicalism, or is it vice versa? The more "evangelicalism" seeks to be cast or accepts being cast as a theo-political brand, the more motivating it is for some evangelicals to walk away from the tribe, not as a rejection of Christian orthodoxy but as a way to preserve and defend it. The alternative is to reclaim evangelical witness as accountable to the righteousness, justice, and mercy of the evangel itself.

WHERE ARE WE?

It has become clear that there are evangelicals and then there are evangelicals. Telling them apart based on certain theological tenets of Christian faith would be difficult, since there are few significant points of distinction. The beliefs about God, Jesus, the Bible, conversion, and the afterlife aren't different enough to explain the growing division between some evangelicals and others.

What divides evangelicals can be found underneath our theology, on the often-recognized mental and social frame on which our theology sits. From conception onward, each of us gradually develops a mental frame that defines our most basic instincts, values, assumptions, habits, and choices. It's as primary as what cues our fears or assuages our anxieties or stimulates our appetites. Our frame tells us "what is" and gives us the impression that it's the baseline of reality itself; it includes unexamined yet gripping "facts."

On top of our frame sits our theological beliefs. Of course, being evangelical typically means belief in theology as the bedrock, not our frame. But what the 2016 US presidential election exposed so vividly is the reverse. Evangelicals can affirm that faith commitments and their implications are essential to discerning values; but when evangelicals who affirm the same baseline of faith reach radically opposing social and political opinions, we have to ask what else is at play. The collision can't be explained by different definitions of the incarnation or by alternate views of the Bible and its authority. Rather, opposing views expose that underneath "one Lord, one faith, one baptism" lie basic instincts in our mental and social frames related to who and what actually matters.

Red and blue states cluster, and with them the churches in those regions. This points to what we could call our theologized ideology—belief that has an attachment to biblical faith but is fundamentally shaped by the social and political mindset in which that faith is nurtured. We see this in current issues that were primed for evangelical responses: conservative social anxiety over an ever-wider reach of an ever-wider liberal and secular government agenda; culture-war debates about abortion and homosexuality and potential Supreme Court nominees; threats to US safety because of terrorism and the role of Islam; economic and social elitism that isolates and ignores the cries and struggles of middle- and lower-class citizens, particularly whites; roiling anger and fear over issues of immigration and race, especially killings of unarmed, young black men, further unsettling a narrative of America as exceptional, Christian, and white. The regionalisms that cast these issues differently are evident in the evangelicalism that emerges within them.

Depending much on our social location, these dramas carry varying importance and meanings. Their urgency and relative priority tends to be a reflection of where we live and a measure of the social anxiety, vulnerability, and pragmatism around us: who and what is at risk, and what price should be paid for defense or change? Our Christian faith speaks to all of these concerns. Yet when our context or ideology leaves us desperate, angry, or fearful, it's more attractive to look for an alternative that asserts whatever populist power we can find.

A middle-class, underemployed, white American, perhaps living in Appalachia or the Rust Belt, may believe failed immigration policy or enforcement has disrupted their "God-given right" to work, which makes it difficult to support welcoming the alien or stranger. An African American or Latino American living in Los Angeles or New York may view huge rallies of white people as excluding or mistreating people who look like them and hear the rallies' language about God as abusive and its "good news" as unrecognizable.

Tensions among faith, context, and action are not new, of course. They permeate the Scripture, the church, and US history. Jesus knew that building a house on rock would never be as easy—and therefore as common—as building on sand. The dilemma of living faith wouldn't be newsworthy now apart from the disjunction that puts evangelical inconsistencies under a hot national spotlight. With the cross of Christ as the theological centerpiece and model of evangelical faith, people inside and outside the church expect evidence of the pursuit of moral purity and/or of the humility of self-sacrifice. Both of these now seem buried in the rhetoric of populist and partisan political power.

Traditional Christian convictions about a comprehensive vision of faithfulness seem to have shrunk in the culture-war battles over abortion and homosexuality, immigration and race. No matter whether the battle involves the evangelical right or left, the gloves have come off, and the battle rages as it will. The incongruous fury or inconsistency that arises is rationalized as the cost of just war, whether for or against these defining issues. Meanwhile, the personal virtues of humility, compassion, and public commitments to justice and righteousness seem to have been submerged by both the church and the media. No evangelicalism is in question; the evangel itself seems to have been marginalized.

Fatigued, angry, and desperate, many white evangelicals, particularly in the central and southern states, made an alliance with the unlikely candidacy of Donald Trump. In an iconoclastic and populist eruption of desire for ideological change in our national narrative around issues of class, race, gender, religion, government, nation, and globalization, 81 percent of white evangelicals reportedly voted in support of Trump. Many white evangelicals voted out of protest and rejection of the liberalizing effects of the Democratic Party, and particularly of Hilary Clinton. Noted white evangelical voices spoke vehemently against Trump's candidacy on grounds of competence and suitability. Nonetheless, Trump lost the popular vote but won the electoral college and became the forty-fifth president of the United States.

For some evangelicals, this was an agonizing compromise vote, performed as an act of opposition to Hilary Clinton as much or more as support for Donald Trump. However, for many other evangelicals, the vote signified a collective unity and spiritual victory that had at last won a cultural moment, defeating liberal Democrats and asserting their cry for radical change. Such voters celebrated a new American political landscape with a white Republican coming to the White House, accompanied by largely white and Republican Senate and House majorities as well. The prospect of a similar Supreme Court nominee was hugely relieving.

However, this new day of hope for some evangelicals signaled an apocalypse for other evangelicals. The ease with which some on the right could affirm an evangelical faith connected to campaign rhetoric that was racist, sexist, and nationalist was disorienting to an extreme. It left many evangelical people of color gasping in despair and disorientation that so many white brothers and sisters in Christ could vote for someone whose words and actions were so overtly inconsistent with their common faith in Christ. But likewise, the willingness of other evangelicals on the left to tolerate advocacy for abortion rights, same-sex marriage, and a pervasively secular vision for America caused many white evangelicals, even with a troubled conscience, to do anything to stop the liberal political machine. Since the inauguration, the divide between these groups of evangelicals has revealed just how deep the lines of distrust and disassociation across the evangelical political and social spectrums are.

Feelings and rhetoric flow passionately along these two opposing sides of the evangelical community, separating them with an enormous gulf of theologized ideology. Security for some means intensified fear for others. For many, feelings of finally being seen and heard left others feeling stalked and targeted. Class, race, and gender issues tore the fabric of evangelicalism, perhaps irrecoverably. What emerged was a deep separation because of social location, personal experience, and spiritual conviction, even if the "sides" held a similar view of Jesus, eternal salvation, and biblical authority. A house divided indeed.

Abortion, homosexuality, race, and immigration are some of the biggest social dangers in the minds of many white evangelicals. These are important social ethics issues, and the Christian faith can and should inform our way of understanding each of them. But typically, before that exploration even gets under way, our sociology presets our convictions before the teaching of the Bible has been considered and integrated into our lives. And this can be as true of the right as it is of the left. This doesn't minimize the potential for biblical faith to inform our social location, particularly about important matters such as these. It is striking, however, that our context is the most pervasive influence that shapes us, even if we profess Jesus as Lord. The red-and-blue-state pattern reflects the profound sway of social location.

The denial of personal racism by many in the evangelical right is often paired with blindness toward systemic racism. This combination continues to play out in familiar but devastating ways for many evangelical African Americans, Latinos, and others. The evangelical right's sustained failure to demonstrate the theological and spiritual capacity to grapple with a long history of racial abuse—for which white Christians in America bear particular guilt (from the beginnings of slavery to police shootings of unarmed black men)—has led many evangelical Christians, both white and people of color, to dissociate from evangelicalism. For them, white supremacy and white evangelicalism are synonymous and equally unacceptable.

Until the previous decade, the overwhelming percentage of evangelicals would have reliably and consistently defended a traditional view of marriage as a relationship between a man and a woman, and maintained that homosexual activity is outside the bounds of biblical ethics. In the last decade, this consensus has eroded in two directions: geographical and generational. As the East and West Coasts of the United States have led the way in the growing affirmation of LGBT people and lifestyles, evangelicals in these regions have quietly done likewise. When the Supreme Court affirmed same-sex marriage, the state debates and votes ceased, and a lot of evangelicals accepted the legal status and legitimacy of same-sex relationships. Perhaps even more noteworthy is the generational divide over the acceptance of LGBT relationships, with affirmation from 47 percent of white evangelicals under the age of thirty, despite their otherwise more traditional views. Their cultural frame led to a recasting of their faith understanding.

Such a tense and wracking division within an influential theological and religious sector of Christian America underscores a far more profound set of issues than mere arguments between conservatives and progressives. A pure Christian identity isn't available, because we all live immersed in context. But evangelical language easily falls prey to making absolutist statements in ways that appear to claim a biblical "purity" of vision unfettered by anything other than the Bible. Meanwhile, what mystifies and infuriates the evangelical left is that the voice of the evangelical right seems to be controlled by white supremacy, moral and political inconsistency, and a fearful nationalism and isolationism that bears little evidence of the fruit of God's Spirit. Again, social frame matters in how we see and what we see.

EVANGELICALISM AND THE PUBLIC SQUARE

In its larger historical context, contemporary evangelicalism is a relative newcomer to the public square. The emergence of the Moral Majority in the late seventies introduced conservative Christian politics to the national scene. Jimmy Carter complicated the picture a bit by being a pious Baptist, a Bible-focused Sunday school teacher, and a Democrat from Georgia. By contrast, the primary thrust of the Moral Majority was white Republicanism on the religious right.

Over the intervening decades, the Moral Majority (more fundamentalist than evangelical) defined faith and the public square in ways that were politically conservative, issue centered, and largely bombastic and hostile toward culture and government. Out of this context, the term *culture wars* emerged and gradually became identified as the evangelical posture toward the public square.

This continues in the voices of many in the evangelical right, and the binary nature of the culture wars has made it difficult for any who dare to call themselves the evangelical left to avoid being lambasted as heretics or frauds by the evangelical right. Rather than seeing the public square as a context for substantial and civil discussions of issues of faith and society, the rhetoric has operated more like an on-off, right-wrong switch. This has greatly intensified passions and hasn't enhanced public discussion or the need for a more careful and diverse set of Christian voices to be heard in the public square.

The 2016 election extended this situation further while opting for pragmatic power (by which Trump is compared to Cyrus, the pagan king used by God for holy ends) rather than coherent piety (as seen by the endorsement of Trump despite his lack of what would usually be considered "Christian" character qualities).

Each believer occupies and is occupied by a social context—that is, an educational, economic, racial, and religious ethos that permeates and shapes each of us. We are never context-free. Context sets our life's terms and possibilities; it is the frame that defines, supports, and contradicts our values and actions. A confession of trusting in Jesus as Savior and Lord has to be worked into every dimension of our life—formed and socialized as we are in light of everything from our genes to our family, race, class, education, and more.

Common evangelical faith claims confidence and trust in the supracultural good news of Jesus Christ that makes a first-order claim on what is true and most important. As Savior and Lord, no one and nothing rivals Jesus Christ. But what does that primary evangelical affirmation mean for embodied daily life in Biloxi or Madison, San Francisco or Chicago?

When evangelicals went to the polls on November 8, 2016, we presumably went as people trusting Jesus Christ and praying for God's will. We hopefully thought and prayed carefully about our choices as we voted. What we may not have done was make an effort to examine carefully how our choices were influenced by Jesus and the kingdom he came to preach and establish. We may not have asked how we'd been shaped by our context and culture or asked whether we were using Jesus as leverage based on our social location.

EVANGELICALISM AND KINGDOM SOCIOLOGY

All of these factors contribute to the divided evangelicalism of this season. For those on the evangelical right, the pragmatic political outcomes of the election and its aftermath may seem to be grounds for justifying their tactics and protecting their religious brand. It remains to be seen whether such results occur. Even if they don't, the fallback posture is simply that sometimes "the bad guys" win, and the just-war battle moves ahead as "the good guys" soldier on.

What such an approach would likely *not* do, however, is engage in constructive self-critique, including a deep reexamination of the relationship between evangelical theological identity and social location or ideology. Circling the wagons is a more likely strategy, and that won't lead to change but to retrenchment, whether of the right or the left.

If this is so, it's likely many on the evangelical left will more completely and broadly disassociate from the culture, churches, and institutions that have become known as white evangelicalism. As the racial diversity and generational differences among evangelical churches on the left continue to grow, it will become more and more unpalatable to choose association with evangelicals on the right. It will feel like a choice between bigotry and justice, in which case faith and social location will compel the evangelical left toward justice.

In the New Testament letter to the Ephesians, the apostle Paul argues that the Ephesians were spiritually dead but were made alive in and through Jesus Christ. This language and affirmation lies at the very core of the Christian gospel, and it's the way evangelicals have articulated and proclaimed the good news. So far, so good. However, what Paul goes on to describe is exceptionally important yet uncomfortable for many white American evangelicals: though we were once dead but now alive, the evidence of our resurrected life is our participation in a resurrection community of not-alike people, who in Christ are now made into one new humanity.

In other words, the trajectory of salvation leads to a new sociology—a new social location and communion that is made possible only because of Jesus, who brings divided enemies into one new social reality. This is the pragmatic evidence that the gospel is true; it provides the sign of what only God could do in a broken, divided, warring world. The God of shalom has made peace, and the sign of that is an unexpected new community between unlike people who may even have been enemies.

This is the agenda and burden, the promise and hope that a full evangelicalism should speak and demonstrate. Sadly, when evangelicals truncate the gospel and focus on personal and spiritual transformation without communal, systemic, and public transformation, we find ourselves just where we are: reproducing the same social locations and ideology as when we were "dead in [our] trespasses." We may try to say we have been "made alive" (Ephesians 2:1 NKJV), but whenever we show little or no interest in working out the social implications of this new identity and life in Christ, is it any wonder that our witness is confusing and unconvincing?

In an era of declining church attendance in the United States, allegiances to congregations and denominations are waning significantly. Evangelical churches as well as mainline congregations are diminishing, and the growing number of disaffected youth and young adults is frequently noted.[1]

The social battering of Christian orthodoxy is not new, but the crisis facing the evangelical church as a result of the 2016 election and its aftermath is a problem of our own doing. It exposes issues that haven't been taken up with adequate faith or action. For the evangelical witness in the United States to flourish, it doesn't need better branding but genuine revival: the personal and social transformation that more fully bears witness to the adequacy, truth, and relevance of the gospel of Jesus Christ. Issues will continue to be more about social location than theology proper, and efforts to live a gospel that humbly and authentically reflects the sociology of the kingdom of God will continue to call out to those who have "ears to hear" (a term Jesus used often).

STILL EVANGELICAL OR YET EVANGELICAL?

It may be a very evangelical act to decide whether one is truly evangelical. The rife individualism of evangelicalism is obvious these days. The decision to be in or be out of the tribe will no doubt continue to shift in light of various factors— not least being the relationship between evangelicalism and political rhetoric.

The future of American Christianity will be affected by the current and future dynamics of evangelicalism, arguably one of its most vibrant and determined movements. Its multidenominational and nondenominational expressions mean it has plenty of room for flexibility and change—qualities that are among its most distinctive.

The highest reputed value in evangelicalism is the gospel itself—the only good news that can finally change the world. Thus the hope and corrective, to the right or left of evangelicalism, is that the evangel can and must continue to change evangelicalism itself. Whether "still evangelical" or not, being open and responsive to gospel transformation in word and deed is the most evangelical thing one can do.

Evangelical has value only if it names our commitment to seek and to demonstrate the heart and mind of God in Jesus Christ, who is the evangel. To be evangelical is to respond to God's call into deeper faith and greater humility. It also leads us to repudiate and resist all forces of racism and misogyny, and all other attitudes and actions, overt and implied, that subvert the dignity of people, who are made in the image of God. The evangel holds our evangelicalism to account and not vice versa.

The only evangelicalism worthy of its name must be one that both faithfully points to and mirrors Jesus Christ. It is the good news for the world as it seeks justice that reflects the character of God's kingdom. Any evangelicalism that seeks its own power is unfaithful to the evangel it claims to represent. Any evangelicalism that doesn't allow the evangel to redefine, reorder, and renew power in light of Jesus Christ is lost and worth abandoning.

Referring to oneself as evangelical is not a congratulatory self-description (as though it were a trophy), nor a theo-political brand (as though it were a platform). It is rather a commitment and an aspiration to identify with God's great love in Christ and, in true humility, to cry out for the daunting and urgent hope we believe can transform us and transform our world. It is a call to acknowledge and repent of our complicity in sin and injustice (both personal and systemic), and to work toward the reordering of all power after Jesus' example. It's a vision of living with coherence and integrity so that we truthfully proclaim and faithfully enact God's good news of love, justice, and mercy in Jesus Christ.

If this is what the word *evangelical* means, then perhaps the pressing question is not, *Still evangelical?* but rather, *Yet evangelical?*

1

WILL EVANGELICALISM SURRENDER?

LISA SHARON HARPER

Brown knees kiss earth, head bends in contrition, elbows balance a hunched body at the altar as tears fall. The itinerant preacher warned of hellfire and brimstone that Sunday night, August 21, 1983. He preached for what seemed like forever. I barely remember a word of his sermon now, except that I was in danger of hell because I had not given my life to Jesus.

It had been a yearlong journey from autumn 1982 to August 1983—a journey with a single purpose: to know Jesus and God and figure out how to pray. I had attended two all-white local youth groups where I did walk-a-thons and sing-a-thons for Jesus and committed whole passages of Scripture to memory. I went to Michael Card, Amy Grant, Michael W. Smith, and even Stryper concerts. Yes, this African American fourteen-year-old cut bangs that stuck straight out from my forehead. I donned black eyeliner inside the eyelid, according to local Cape May fashion. It mattered not that my mother helped establish the Philadelphia office of Student Nonviolent Coordinating Committee in the 1960s. It mattered not that she dated the man who coined the phrase "Black Power." No, I banged my head with extra passion during the heavy-metal Stryper concert. I made sure I belonged.

As the organ bellowed at that Sunday-evening camp church meeting, my friend Terry tapped me on the shoulder and asked whether I would go to the altar with her.

I nodded. I had wanted to go—had toyed with tapping her shoulder—but I was too chicken.

We both walked forward. We both knelt in the dust. We both wept. We were both surrounded and prayed for. She was already a Christian. I never knew why she wept. In fact, I never knew why I wept that night, except that saying yes to Jesus felt like surrender. The tears flowed.

That same year, evangelicalism was experiencing an orchestrated takeover by political operatives of the conservative movement.

The desegregation of public schools served as the backdrop for the conservative movement's takeover and politicization of previously isolationist evangelicals. When black boys and girls began sitting at school desks next to white boys and girls, white parents pulled their sons and daughters out of public schools across the South and Midwest and established what they called "race schools"—all-white schools. Often these schools shielded themselves from government encroachment under the First Amendment protection of religious freedom.

In Michael Cromartie's *No Longer Exiles*, a conservative operative and architect of the rise of the religious right in the late 1970s named Paul Weyrich explains that the political evangelical movement was a movement on the defensive against government encroachment. "What caused the movement to surface," he said at an exclusive Washington, DC, meeting of religious-right leaders in 1990, was part of "the federal government's moves against Christian schools. This absolutely shattered the Christian community's notion that Christians could isolate themselves inside their own institutions and teach what they pleased."[1]

After the foundation of the Fourteenth Amendment, the affirmation of judicial law established under *Brown v. Board of Education of Topeka* in 1954, and the legislative enforcement established by the Civil Rights Act of 1964, African American parents in Mississippi filed a class-action lawsuit in 1970 against race schools that had attempted to subvert desegregation while maintaining tax-exempt status. These Mississippi parents won their case: *Green v. Connally*. The same year, the IRS informed Bob Jones University that its tax-exempt status would be revoked because of its segregationist policies.

In *Thy Kingdom Come*, Randall Balmer recounts the meeting where Weyrich spoke in 1990. Balmer recalls that someone tried to make the point that abortion was the catalyst for the rise of the right. Weyrich voiced staunch opposition to the notion, insisting, "What got us going as a political movement was the attempt on the part of the Internal Revenue Service (IRS) to rescind the tax-exempt status of Bob Jones University because of its racially discriminatory policies."[2]

Weyrich explains in *No Longer Exiles* that the moment the evangelical movement consummated its covenant relationship with the conservative movement was the moment when the notion that they could isolate themselves in their own institutions "linked up with the long held conservative view that government is too powerful and intrusive." Weyrich says this link made evangelicals active. "It wasn't the abortion issue. That wasn't sufficient."[3]

The same year that my brown knees knelt at a dusty campground altar, the Supreme Court issued its verdict on Bob Jones
University: it sided against the university and finally revoked its
tax-exempt status—completely.

As tears of contrition fell from my African American eyes onto
the old wooden altar in the center of the South Jersey Tabernacle
United Methodist campground, white Southern and Midwestern
evangelicals were rising in protest of government infringement
on their religious liberties. Buzzwords of the conservative
movement were adopted as battle cries of the evangelical revolt:
"Small government!" "Religious freedom!" "Traditional values!"
These words flew from the lips of the same women and men that
only twenty years earlier might not have felt compelled to shroud
their language in the niceties of political correctness. They might
have yelled, "States' rights!" "N----- lover!" "Segregation forever!"

The new language didn't just appear. It was cultivated. Propa-
ganda was distributed to evangelical churches during Reagan's
1984 run for a second term. As I walked out of the white steepled
tabernacle of my own Erma, New Jersey, church and into the
crisp rural air one Sunday night, I was handed a tract. It looked
like the tracts we handed out on the boardwalk—the kind with
comic-strip illustrations that call sinners to repent, believe, and
be saved. But this tract warned that Mondale was the antichrist.
If Mondale won, all the little children would be rounded up in
work camps, and Christianity would be outlawed.

It was brilliant. It hit every conservative note in the key of
E-vangelical. Reagan won by a landslide, and political conservatism became the official ideology of evangelicalism.

■ ■ ■

The Justice Conference was established in Bend, Oregon, by Ken Wytsma in 2010. One evangelical church was attempting to help a new generation of evangelicals grasp the biblical call for justice in the context of the scandal-ridden fall of the religious right's old guard in 2006 and the rise of the first African American president, Barack Obama, two years later. Justice was suddenly cool, but it had shallow roots.

What could one expect? Southern evangelicals had spent the first part of the twentieth century arguing to protect states' rights and keep lynching legal.[4] Evangelicals in the Midwest and South spent the second half of the century arguing for smaller government and wars on drugs that morphed into wars on black communities—complete with demands for law and order, mandatory minimums, and three-strikes laws that snatched 1.5 million black men and boys from their families.

The same evangelicals journaled self-centered prayers at Starbucks while pledging allegiance to conservative pacts with private prison companies and refusals to pass immigration reform. They controlled, confined, and exploited the labor of black and brown bodies behind bars as if they were antebellum chattel. Then, suddenly, after thirty years of refusing to pass immigration reform or an equal-rights amendment, declaring AIDS as God's judgment on gay people and 9/11 as God's judgment because of gay people, voting in tax cuts for the top 1 percent while cutting food assistance for those Jesus called "the least of these," and after more than a century defending and securing white male supremacy, America elected a black president.

In September 2009, I watched, drop-jawed, as Rep. Joe Wilson (R-SC) yelled, "You lie!" during President Obama's address to a joint session of Congress on health care.[5] (He later said he had let his emotions get away from him.)

In March 2010, I watched legendary House members Rep. Emmanuel Cleaver and Rep. John Lewis pass through jeering crowds of white Tea Party members, flanked by capitol police. The crowd covered Lewis in racial epithets and spat on Rep. Cleaver.[6] It reminded me of Elizabeth Eckford and the Little Rock Nine's long walk to their high school—through the jeering crowd of angry white women, men, and children flanked by city police.

In this context, the Justice Conference was conceived and born. Justice was sexy to white evangelical millennials, but it had absolutely no connection to the ongoing struggles of African Americans, Native Americans, poor people, women, immigrants, and the LGBT community in their struggles for equal recognition and equal protection of their divine call, and capacity to help steward the world.

Now, seven years after the Justice Conference was founded, more millennial evangelicals have a value for justice. But evangelicals as a whole feel further from justice than ever before.

Evangelicals are the most cohesive voting block of any people group that voted for Donald Trump in the 2016 election.[7] Within Trump's first one hundred days, he issued an executive order that prioritized *all* undocumented immigrants for deportation, regardless of criminal history or status.[8] Within one week in early March 2017, US Immigration and Customs Enforcement (ICE) picked up 161 immigrants on the streets of Los Angeles and deported them all within twenty-four hours without trial or legal representation.[9] Advocates in North Carolina have reported that ICE agents followed school buses to arrest students on their way to school.[10]

Likewise, within days of being sworn in, Attorney General Jeff Sessions issued a statement that his Department of Justice (DOJ) would prioritize the protection of law enforcement officers and stop monitoring troubled police departments.[11] At the same time, he issued directives that instructed his office not to pursue the prosecution of police officers previously under DOJ investigation for the killings of black men, women, and children. Meanwhile, he announced that the Trump administration would reverse the Obama initiative to phase out the federal use of for-profit prisons.[12]

In addition, in response to the Supreme Court's 2013 nullification of section 4 of the Voting Rights Act, previously leashed legislatures across the South and Midwest changed their voting laws and structures to block and suppress the access of African American, Hispanic, Asian, low-income, female, and Muslim voters to the polls. Nearly three hundred thousand voters in Wisconsin alone were blocked from voting in the 2016 election because they lacked the proper ID.[13] In this context, Sessions recently issued directives to the DOJ to halt six years of Obama administration litigation against the state of Texas for its voter suppression laws.[14]

Also, President Trump has twice issued executive orders to prohibit travelers from seven, then six, predominantly Muslim nations from entering the United States. Twice federal courts declared his orders unconstitutional—a breach of the First Amendment right to religious liberty.

In this context, white evangelicals continue to demonstrate either support for or passive indifference toward the administration, which 81 percent of them helped to elect.[15]

■ ■ ■

I sat on the stage during the final panel discussion of the Justice Conference 2017. I wasn't supposed to be there; I wasn't slated to speak. But bestselling author and blogger Ann Voskamp had called me up to take her place. I had watched her and the other panelists take their seats. I had listened intently as she shared about the women she'd just met at a refugee camp in the Middle East. I had watched as tears welled up in her eyes and her voice faltered.

Dr. Christena Cleveland had just given a powerful keynote address explaining to the largely white crowd that Jesus is not into equality but equity. For that reason, she said, there will be those who are first and those who are last. God's call to take the lowest seat is for the redemption and healing of those who have known only the highest; being last is for the healing of white people in the United States.

I watched as Voskamp thanked Cleveland for her message and then asked, "Is Lisa Sharon Harper still in the house?" I raised my hand. Then she did something I'd never witnessed in a white evangelical setting. She said, "I think you should be up here. Please come and take my seat." This tall, white woman with more than ten thousand Twitter followers had decentered herself.

I was still marveling over the prophetic nature of the moment as I looked out over the audience and considered the question "What will justice require of us evangelicals?"

1. We must treat every single human being as created in the image of God. (See Genesis 1:26-27.) Since we are made in the image of God, we are created with the divine call and capacity to exercise stewardship of the world—to protect and serve the world. But through our laws, policies, systems, and structures, we have crafted a world in which we declared some people to be "savages" and others "civilized." By law, we declared that some people are "chattel" and others are full human beings.

Thus, for a full century, immigrants entered the United States and fought their way to the Supreme Court to prove that they were white. Why? Because they didn't like their nationality, their ethnic heritage, their culture? No. It was so they could be counted as fully human—so that they could be counted as white. Only people deemed white by the state were recognized by the law as having the divine call, capacity, and right to steward this land.

Now consider this: the ancients believed the image of the king was a marker of where the king ruled. Wherever the king's image flourished, it was an indicator that the kingdom was flourishing. Wherever the king's image was crushed, mangled, destroyed, it was an indicator that there was war against the king in that land. We are made in the image of God. When we govern in a way that diminishes or crushes the capacity of people or people groups to exercise stewardship of the world, we are diminishing or crushing the image of God on earth. We are setting ourselves up as enemies of the kingdom of God—enemies of God.

Luke set up the beginning of his Gospel in a way that tells us this good news is about the king of the kingdom of God come to earth to confront the kingdoms of men—kingdoms hell-bent on crushing, exploiting, and diminishing the image of God on earth.

Jesus declared in his very first sermon why he came:

The Spirit of the Lord is upon me,
    because he has anointed me
        to bring good news to the poor.

He has sent me to proclaim release to the captives
    and recovery of sight to the blind,

> to let the oppressed go free,
>
> to proclaim the year of the Lord's favor.
>
> (Luke 4:18-19 NRSV)

I believe Jesus came to set the oppressed image of God free on earth. *That* is why justice matters. Justice protects, serves, and cultivates the image of God on earth.

2. We must not confuse compassion with justice. Throughout the conference, stories of compassion were cited and called stories of justice. But we must not confuse compassion and justice. Both are needed, but they are different. Compassion is what happens when we are moved from the bowels to feel as God feels for the suffering of another. It's what happens when we feel what the other feels. It moves us to action to help someone up. It moves us to give of ourselves to stop their suffering.

Justice is what happens when we examine the suffering in our world, find the structural, policy, systemic, social, and personal causes, and work to make the world as it *should* be.

3. We must talk about politics in our churches. Politics, at its essence, is simply the conversations we have and the decisions we make about how the *polis* (the people) will live together. If we fail to have these conversations, we abdicate our calling to govern in a way that protects, serves, and cultivates the image of God on earth. That is our call: to govern in the likeness of God—to be witnesses (evidence) of the presence of the kingdom of God in the world.

Politics put simply is this: an incredibly powerful space where the ethics of the kingdom of God and the kingdoms of humanity are given permission to be lived out in real time and have a real effect on the image of God in our world.

4. We must decolonize our theology. The theologians that most of the Western church exalts as divinely inspired interpreters of

Scripture approach the text from the social location of empire. Yet every single word of every single verse of every single chapter of every single biblical book was by an oppressed person. Even David and Solomon were kings of a small nation that kept falling into war.

Here is the critical question: Is it possible for someone who lives, breathes, and interprets Scripture from the social location of empire to understand a book written entirely from the underside of empire—written by and for oppressed peoples?

All of us, no matter who we are, must decolonize our theology.

5. We must address shame. Fellow speakers and conference attendees alike came to talk with me after the panel. One thing seemed to haunt every white person I talked to: shame. The temptation is to give in to shame. But shame is dangerous. It tells us who we *are* and what we *do*. Shame erases our humanity and makes us only as worthy as the worst thing we've ever done. Shame is a lie.

It's possible to do shameful things. But when the message becomes "I have done shameful things, therefore I am shameful," we are believing a lie, and we are in trouble.

Shame keeps us hiding in the dark. Shame keeps our heads buried in the sand while the world burns around us. Shame prevents us from facing the wrong things we have done—the evil we have complied with and benefited from. Shame tells us it will be better for us if we live the fantasy of perfection. But that's just it. Fantasies always end. Reality always wins.

What if the cost of facing evil (through lament, contrition, loss of control, relinquishing the fantasy of supremacy) is far less than the gain?

What if, by facing the evil, evangelicals deemed "white" by the state unlock a process that reconnects them to their own fleshliness, to their own need for others, to the yearning of their souls for deeper connection—for forgiveness?

What if the process of repentance—restitution and repair—is the way of God, the narrow road to the health of our world?

And what if repentance is the way to the restoration of the image of God in a people group twisted by hubris?

And what if the call of God to white evangelicals is to stop trying to be God, to control everything and everyone, and to join the rest of humanity—beloved dust?

Then the question is this: Will the hope of resurrection be enough to move white evangelicals toward the brown wooden altar? Will the hope of becoming human again lead to bowed heads and hunched bodies, pink knees kissing brown dust? Will lament lead to surrender?

2

WHY I AM AN EVANGELICAL

KAREN SWALLOW PRIOR

More and more, *evangelical* is a contested word. Few seem able to agree on what it means today. Some have rejected what they think the word has come to mean and have said farewell to evangelicalism. As someone who has been evangelical for most of my life, I have at times been frustrated with evangelicalism—and disappointed, too.

Yet I can't quit evangelicalism. Nor do I want to.

While I appreciate and admire much about other Christian traditions—their liturgy, their beauty, their order, and their history—I simply am an evangelical. And there are many reasons why.

I am an evangelical because the movement's origin and defining characteristics are deeply rooted in the Protestant Reformation, which defines the core tenets of my Christian belief. While I value much of the beauty, liturgy, and sacramentalism of other Christian traditions, the theology of the Reformation is essential to my Christian belief. The five *solas* of the Reformation are well known:

- *Sola Scriptura:* Scripture alone is the highest authority of the faith.
- *Sola fide:* Faith alone in Jesus Christ saves us.
- *Sola gratia:* The grace of God alone grants saving faith.
- *Solus Christus:* Jesus Christ alone is our Savior.
- *Soli Deo gloria:* We exist for the glory of God alone.

The path from the Reformation to evangelicalism is fairly straight. In fact, Martin Luther referred to the Protestant church as the "evangelical church" to distinguish it from the Catholic Church, from which it broke away. However, the split from Rome was slow in places, sometimes more of a splintering than a snap. This is particularly true of the English Reformation, which is the most direct line to modern-day American evangelicalism.

Too often evangelicalism in total—now a two-centuries-old global movement—is conflated with twenty-first-century American evangelicalism. This equation often underlies the criticism of those disgruntled by evangelicalism today. It's easy to associate evangelicalism strictly with American Christianity. But it's wrong to do so, on several counts, beginning with the most well-known and universally accepted definition of evangelicalism, which comes from the historian David Bebbington in his 1989 book *Evangelicalism in Modern Britain: A History from the 1730s to the 1980s.* He identified four defining characteristics as central to evangelicalism, from its beginnings and continuing through today. These four characteristics have come to be known as the Bebbington Quadrilateral:

- biblicism: placement of ultimate authority in Scripture, a particular regard for the Bible

- crucicentrism: emphasis on the atonement achieved by Christ's crucifixion
- conversionism: centrality of the conversion experience (being "born again") to salvation
- activism: belief that the gospel has implications for how one lives in and affects the world[1]

I first read Bebbington's book about ten years after its publication. By then I was pretty firmly established within my evangelical identity, but it was the first time I had encountered an objective and scholarly account of who *I* was—or so it seemed to me. (What could be more evangelical than reading myself as an individual agent into the pages of the book?) Further, the centrality of the Bible for doctrine and practice, the emphasis on Christ's sacrifice on the cross for my sins, my long identification as someone who had been born again, the political and social activism that had marked my coming of age—all explained my faith in a way that helped me understand not just who I was but also how I had come to be.

I am evangelical because evangelicalism is apt for the modern age. While the evangelical movement began just about two hundred years ago, its long roots in the Protestant Reformation mean that, as much as—or even more than—anything else, evangelicalism has helped to define the modern age. Indeed, evangelicalism is, for good and ill, the quintessential expression of Christianity for modernity.

Despite some declarations of the death of modernity and, with it, evangelicalism, the fact is that no age or its ethos ever vanishes. Whatever the earthly future holds for the church and human culture, evangelicalism and modernity will be carried into it. Whatever postmodernity and postevangelicalism are, they are because of modernity. And despite shifts in style, the substance of both evangelicalism and modernity are very much with us still.

What exactly is modernity? It's most succinctly defined as a turn to the subject—or, in other words, a turn from an objective, universal authority (such as a pope or a monarch). It's encapsulated in René Descartes's decree, "I think, therefore I am." With this and other important developments beginning around the sixteenth century, the locus of truth, being, and knowledge shifted, becoming primarily internal rather than external. This modern subjectivity led to the rise of the individual and to a new sense of selfhood, something we moderns take for granted (and can't even imagine existing without) because we are, well, modern.

Modernity is inseparable from the Protestant Reformation and the evangelicalism the Reformation birthed. The *solas* of the Reformation find a natural culmination in evangelicalism's emphasis on the individual, which manifests in numerous ways.

In evangelicalism, Christian belief is affirmed by personal experience, whether personal reading of Scripture or personal conversion and subsequent leading of the Holy Spirit (a feature of evangelicalism that historian Thomas Kidd has suggested to be a notable omission from Bebbington's Quadrilateral[2]). The ultimate authority of the Bible is manifested in the life of the individual believer through the reading of the Word, not through the mediation of a pope or priest. Conversion occurs by individual will (even if predestined) and is not counted merely by circumstances of birth. The Holy Spirit teaches, comforts, and counsels on an individual as well as a communal basis.

Part of what it means to live and worship as a Christian within the church but without an external human authority such as a pope results, necessarily, in some groping and faltering as we figure out what faithfulness looks like in different times and different ages. This is a tension as fraught with risk as it is with opportunity for growth. But this challenging nature of the faith is the very thing that makes it exciting and worthwhile. Robust Christianity is not for the faint of heart—or the faint of mind. Yet, paradoxically, we must become like children in order to come into this faith. The challenge of this paradox is most vibrant within evangelicalism, where trials foster both the responsibilities of the individual and the call of the community.

Community is manifested within evangelicalism not only within the congregation of each church but also through evangelicalism's connection to the birth of the modern social conscience. The very idea that people could—and should—change social conditions for the better is the fruit of the evangelical movement. The Age of Progress, as the eighteenth and nineteenth centuries came to be known, resulted from the spirit of reform birthed and matured by early evangelicalism.[3]

This spirit of reform and, along with it, the spirit of the modern individual found their expression in a new literary genre in the eighteenth century: the novel. Both evangelicalism and the rise of the individual contributed immeasurably to the development of this literary genre most characteristic of modernity. The novel and the eighteenth-century period that birthed it are the areas of my own academic specialty. And despite being raised in evangelical churches, it was not until I was immersed in my doctoral studies in the English novel that I learned this important and compelling chapter on evangelicalism and its role in the modern world. Now I can't separate my study of and love for the period from myself.

Both evangelicalism and the novel are expressions of the rise of the individual as a concept and as a lived experience characteristic of modernity. From the antifiction of John Bunyan's allegory *The Pilgrim's Progress* to the journalistic-style fiction of Daniel Defoe to the Methodism of Samuel Richardson's *Pamela* (which many scholars consider the first novel in English) to Jane Austen's *Mansfield Park,* the evangelical movement has its fingerprints all over the earliest English novels.

Furthermore, the spirit of activism (one-fourth of Bebbington's Quadrilateral) inspired the social critique that defines nearly all the great Victorian novels, particularly those of Victorian novelist Charles Dickens. The social consciousness that characterizes the world of Dickens's novels—sensitivity to the plights of the orphan, the poverty-stricken, and the dehumanized victims of the Industrial Revolution—was the fruit of the evangelical spirit of reform and revival.

Modernity surely has its faults and limits, and the more modernity passes into history, the more clearly those problems can be seen. Still, the modern age has brought many gifts to humankind: the Reformation, the printing press, the scientific method, the rise of the individual, and even the very notion of progress and improvement of the human lot. Evangelicalism has been both the product and the perpetuation of many of the things that make modernity all that it is.

I am evangelical because of the faithful and beautiful witness of our evangelical forebears. One major tributary of the evangelical stream flows from the Puritans. In the seventeenth century, preacher and writer John Bunyan was an important forebear to the movement, as he chose imprisonment over silence when his preaching as a dissenter contradicted English law. He is one of the early examples of an activist Christian with a fierce and thorough commitment to the doctrine of salvation by grace alone and the implication of that belief for every aspect of life—from his preaching to his imprisonment to his writing. He is most famous for *The Pilgrim's Progress*, one of the world's literary masterpieces and one of the most widely read works of Christian literature in all of history.

In the century after Bunyan, England's first evangelicals sought to reclaim and strengthen within the established church (the one brought about by the English Reformation) the purity of doctrine and the piety of holy living that should be the aim of every Christian in all times and all places. To read the sermons of John Wesley, widely considered the father of evangelicalism, is to marvel at the sound wisdom, reliance on God rather than self, and lack of political maneuvering so common within evangelicalism today. Consider this passage from Wesley's sermon "The Nature of Enthusiasm," which cautions against the spirit that has come to characterize so much of evangelical discourse today:

> Beware you are not a fiery, persecuting enthusiast. Do not imagine that God has called you (just contrary to the spirit of Him you style your Master) to destroy men's lives, and not to save them. Never dream of forcing men into the ways of God. Think yourself, and let think. Use no constraint in matters of religion. Even those who are farthest out of the way never compel to come in by any other means than reason, truth, and love.[4]

Particularly lovely is the fact that one of the most beloved poets of the age that birthed evangelicalism was an evangelical. Along with volumes of poetry, William Cowper composed hymns with his friend John Newton, the former slave-ship captain who composed "Amazing Grace." Cowper's poetry, which drew on the neoclassical tradition while brilliantly anticipating the Romantic period, was infused with the evangelical faith that served as his refuge from debilitating depression and his inspiration for finding beauty even in a fallen world. His verse is gorgeous and intense, filled with empathy for slaves and animals and all those who suffered during what was, by most any standard, a coarse age.

Evangelicals also played a central role in the abolition of the British slave trade, including William Wilberforce and Hannah More. Wilberforce, a member of Parliament, spearheaded the political opposition to chattel slavery for the several decades it took to outlaw slavery throughout the British Empire. Wilberforce was the most visible member of the English evangelical reform movement, but he worked closely with many others to bring about this and many other improvements for the greater social good from the latter half of the eighteenth century until his death in 1833. The workings of Wilberforce's rigorous mind are on display in the volumes of journals he kept over a number of years. These journals display beauty of both thought and spirit as the young Wilberforce first struggled with disbelief and then conviction and then saw the fulfillment of God's call on his life.

One of Wilberforce's dearest friends was Hannah More, an evangelical Anglican who partnered with him on numerous reform projects, including abolition and the establishment of some of the earliest Sunday schools. Before coming under the influence of evangelicalism, More was a much-feted poet and dramatist whose work was admired by literary critic Samuel Johnson and stage producer David Garrick, among many other members of the London literati. She wrote some of England's earliest bestsellers and elevated the moral status of the novel, paving the way for the great Victorian novels.[5]

On the other side of the Atlantic, Jonathan Edwards was one of the brightest thinkers and most solid sources of Christian doctrine in history, both in evangelicalism and in the church as a whole. His preaching precipitated a revival so great it led to America's Great Awakening. In Edwards's sermons are the height of the union of reason and poetry:

> God is the highest good of the reasonable creature. The enjoyment of him is our proper happiness; and is the only happiness with which our souls can be satisfied.
>
> To go to heaven, fully to enjoy God, is infinitely better than the most pleasant accommodations here. Better than fathers and mothers, husbands, wives or children, or the company of any, or all earthly friends. These are but shadows; but the enjoyment of God is the substance. These are but scattered beams; but God is the sun. These are but streams; but God is the fountain. These are but drops; but God is the ocean.[6]

If we don't associate such sophistication and eloquence with twenty-first-century evangelicalism, we can't attribute that to our forebears.

Hymnody is another art in which evangelicals have excelled. John Wesley's brother Charles published thousands of hymns in his lifetime, and many are ones still beloved and sung today, including "Christ the Lord Is Risen Today," "O for a Thousand Tongues to Sing," and "And Can It Be That I Should Gain?" The nineteenth-century American hymnist Fanny Crosby not only wrote many hymns that remain popular today but was an accomplished poet and author of many secular songs as well.

Despite the anti-intellectualism that later came to be associated (justly so) with evangelicalism,[7] the movement's earliest forebears were accomplished thinkers. And despite some personal imperfections and cultural blind spots these founders of the movement had (such as George Whitefield's support of slavery), their commitment to pursue orthodoxy and orthopraxy offers a model that serves as both an example and a corrective for us today. We too should pursue orthodoxy and orthopraxy, reminded by the cultural blind spots of our forebears that we are no more immune than they to falling short.

I am evangelical because of the role evangelicalism had in advancing freedom and equality for all people. In his *Thoughts upon Slavery*, John Wesley boldly declared, "Liberty is the right of every human creature, as soon as he breathes the vital air; and no human law can deprive him of that right which he derives from the law of nature."[8] It's not that Christianity promises believers good things such as freedom and equality. By no means. But inasmuch as Christianity aligns with the nature of the created order and the supernatural revelation of God to his people, then the promotion of that good news to all people (that is, evangelism) and the application of those truths (activism) advances the flourishing of God's creation even amid its fallenness.

While we who live in the latter years of modernity can see more clearly the dangers that accompany too much emphasis on the individual and subjectivity (culminating as they now have into a deadly embrace of radical autonomy), the gift of liberty cultivated by evangelicalism far outweighs the risks that accompany it. Responsibility comes with freedom, so the elevation of the individual is accompanied by a corresponding need to hold freedom in balance with a proper understanding of humans as social beings who live in community. We can see this point better now, from our vantage point within late modernity, as the pendulum swings away from too much emphasis on individualism.

Yet even as we correct for one extreme, we dare not forget that the emphasis the early evangelicals placed on each individual arose from their good and true belief in the equal worth and dignity of each human soul. Richardson, the eighteenth-century English novelist mentioned above, helped to advance this evangelical notion of equality in his hugely popular works. In his first novel, *Pamela; or, Virtue Rewarded,* the titular character, a lowborn servant girl, has the audacity to declare (in defense of her stolid resistance of her master's sexual advances), "O Sir! my soul is of equal Importance with the Soul of a Princess; though my Quality is inferior to that of the meanest Slave."[9] The fictional Pamela's words are uttered within the context of sexual and bodily integrity, but her plight as an utterly powerless servant girl hounded and harassed by her wealthy master is not unlike that of the slave. While Wesley sought freedom for African slaves, Richardson advanced the freedom of individual autonomy, both in general and within the context of marriage.

Marriage is another area that evangelicalism profoundly shaped. Evangelicals, and the early novelists who believed in evangelical principles, advanced a vision of marriage as an institution designed to enable both husband and wife to serve in Christian ministry both within the home and without. This understanding

transformed the institution of marriage from one based on political and economic expediency (the joining of ancestral lineages
or landholdings) to one based on personal suitability.

Evangelicals called this the companionate marriage, a union
of the couple's choosing rather than the parents' based on
mutual compatibility in order that both partners might better
fulfill the callings of their earthly ministry. Some of the most
important early novels dealt directly with the marriage question,
challenging with their marriage plots the old narrative, which
upheld marriage as strictly a financial transaction that required
parental approval (and often arrangement). Under the influence
of evangelical ideas, eighteenth- and nineteenth-century novels
helped revolutionize the social imaginary concerning marriage.

The reforming spirit doing battle with slavery, which persisted
over several decades, was expansive enough to address numerous
other issues as well. The evangelical abolitionists sought and
enacted reforms in education, child labor, animal welfare, and
other social arenas. Such activism inadvertently carved out new
spaces for women, too, and ultimately the evangelical movement
increased the authority of women to speak on matters of moral,
social, and religious concern, granting women greater roles in
public life as evangelicals sought to advance the public good.[10]

Some of those quitting evangelicalism today do so, seemingly,
from embarrassment and shame over the way evangelicalism
looks today reflected in the distorted glass held up by media and
poorly designed polls. A greater understanding of evangelicalism's history—and its fruit yet to come from that history—
renders such a view as misguided and shortsighted. While some
fields fall fallow now and then, the rich soil of evangelicalism is,
I firmly believe, yet fertile.

I am evangelical because evangelicalism is my family's faith tradition. When I was born, my parents belonged to the Methodist Church, as my grandparents before them had. I was baptized as a Methodist after accepting Christ as my savior when I was a small child. Shortly after my baptism, however, my family began to attend an evangelical Baptist church. By the time I was a young teen, I was teaching Sunday school to the little ones in the tiny Baptist church we attended in rural Maine. I also helped run games at Vacation Bible School, joined the youth group, assisted with the bus ministry—and got completely burned out by the time I was in my mid-twenties.

Not long after that, and perhaps not surprisingly, I wanted out. I wanted to be Episcopalian. I fell in love with the liturgy. I fell in love with the music sung from behind, where it was heard, not seen. I took the membership classes, but I got hung up on doctrine. I was, I finally had to admit, not Episcopalian but evangelical. I was—and am—Baptist, through and through. I returned to the evangelical Baptist tradition of my youth. It was in this tradition that I came to maturity, grew in my faith, and married. It is in this tradition I remain.

I once read something (somewhere I can no longer remember by someone I also can't remember) stating, essentially, that one should not leave the faith tradition of one's birth unless for a good reason. I've never forgotten this wisdom, which goes against the grain of today's radical autonomy. A person being born into a family, tradition, and culture is an act of God, for God knits soul and body together in a particular womb, in a particular time, and in a particular place. Because of the place, time, and family in which God chose to place me, there is too much of evangelicalism in me, and too much of me in it, to call it quits.

I am evangelical because evangelicalism was profoundly formative in my life, and I want to help form evangelicalism now and for the future. As explained above, I came to Christian belief at a very young age and never wavered in my faith or in my trust in Jesus as my Savior. Sadly, the message that came across within my evangelical tradition was that while trusting in Jesus ensured I would go to heaven instead of hell, there didn't seem to be much else to it beyond that—other than avoiding sin in order to get more jewels in my heavenly crown—and, of course, telling as many other people as I could about Jesus so they could go to heaven and wear a jeweled crown one day, too. This is the shallowness of evangelicalism that I and many others know well.

But a more mature, robust evangelicalism eventually taught me how to think and love like a Christian, too. It taught me what a biblical worldview is. It also showed me the limits of a biblical worldview. Evangelical writers and thinkers helped me face, understand, and challenge the movement's tendency toward anti-intellectualism and its undervaluation of beauty. Evangelicalism eventually taught me that "being saved" was not just about the afterlife but also the abundant life, not just for me as an individual but for all of humankind. Evangelicalism showed me that the truth of God's Word and the message of the gospel make a difference—a powerful difference—in the here and now.

And so evangelicalism created an activist spirit in me, molding and refining a passion to do right politically, socially, personally. The evangelical leaders of the later twentieth century taught and led me in my efforts to promote human life at every stage. And the evangelicals of the eighteenth and nineteenth centuries inspired me to knit those efforts into a holistic pursuit of the flourishing of all human life and God's creation.

Evangelicalism isn't limited to the culture wars in which I came of age or to the rise of the religious right that gave birth to those culture wars. Nor is it tethered inextricably to the evangelicals largely responsible for electing the current US president (an election that uncovered the inherent flaws of a deeply individualistic faith tradition).

I find something powerfully humanizing about facing honestly the weaknesses of my tradition (along with its strength and beauty) and working to overcome those weaknesses from within. Evangelicalism is far deeper, wider, and greater than its particular foibles born of particular times. Like all human works and movements, evangelicalism is far from perfect. In both its history and its present state, there is perhaps too much of the taint of entrepreneurialism, progressivism, and individualism. That some leading evangelicals supported slavery centuries ago while others didn't demonstrates that uniformity, unity, and infallibility are not characteristics of evangelicalism.

I admit that in times of disagreement and injustice, and especially when I have been maligned and attacked by a brother, I have wished for a pope to step in like a father to referee and set things right. Then I remember I have our Father, and he will set all things right in his good time.

Soul freedom is hard. It exacts a great price. Sometimes its toll is deadly. Instead of one human authority over all, we choose instead the individual conscience submitted to the Word and to the Holy Spirit, guided by a community of saints. The price of that freedom is dear, and it is hard. But I believe this is exactly what the call of Christ is for each of us as we work out our salvation in fear and trembling. And, ultimately, that is why I am evangelical.

3

RECAPTURING EVANGELICAL
IDENTITY AND MISSION

MARK YOUNG

ark, why are you an evangelical?" The question caught me
off guard. Asked by a friend, an ordained minister in the
Christian Church (Disciples of Christ) who serves as the executive director of the Interfaith Alliance of Colorado, it
seemed straightforward and based in genuine curiosity. And it
should have been an easy question to answer. But it wasn't. And
it still isn't.

Perhaps a bit of personal history will provide some context
for my dilemma.[1]

I can't recall making a conscious decision to become an evangelical. I was born and raised in a small town in Appalachia and
baptized as a child in the church my family had attended for
years. My faith was in Christ, and my church was American
Baptist. That seemed simple enough. And when my faith commitment was awakened through involvement in Cru and a sense
of calling to ministry took root in my heart and mind, there was

no deep longing to become "an evangelical." In fact, at that time I'm not sure I was even aware of the labels *fundamentalist*, *evangelical*, and *mainline* that had come to define Protestant Christianity in North America.

I became an evangelical by default, I suppose, by choosing to attend the seminary where one of my favorite conference speakers was a faculty member. I knew nothing about that school's place in the constellation of evangelical institutions. Its fundamentalist roots and instincts, along with its emphasis on biblical literalism and apocalypticism, were considered to be normative traits of evangelicalism by those who chose to be a part of that community. I was an eager learner and soaked up the convictions and values of that institution without being aware that it occupied a particularly conservative place on the spectrum of evangelical institutions. Nonetheless, my induction into evangelicalism was *fait accompli*.

Like so many during that era, I became an evangelical and embraced that identity knowing precious little about the history of the movement, its social location in the United States, and its conservative political instincts. For me at that time, an evangelical was simply someone with a testimony of personal faith in the gospel of Jesus Christ who took the Bible seriously, strove to live in line with its teachings, and shared the good news with as many as possible. I don't think I was alone in that understanding.

In the late 1970s, we evangelicals were smug. Those seemed to be the halcyon days of evangelicalism in the United States or, perhaps, to use language more apropos to the popular culture of the times, they were "happy days" for evangelicals. An evangelical had been elected to the Oval Office, a development that caused

Newsweek to dub 1976 "The Year of the Evangelical." Chuck Colson, of Watergate infamy, had published his bestselling testimony of being born again while in prison, and secular media were paying attention to the movement.[2] Furthermore, student ministries, evangelical publishing houses, evangelical contemporary Christian music groups, and media outlets were thriving.

In the echo chamber of the theologically conservative seminary I was attending, it was common knowledge that evangelical ministries and churches were growing while theologically liberal mainline denominations were in decline. And we confidently espoused among ourselves the reason for that phenomenon: evangelicals were committed to preaching the gospel of Jesus Christ, and liberal Christians had abandoned that gospel for social and political action.

Francis Schaeffer's widely influential 1975 book, *How Should We Then Live? The Rise and Decline of Western Thought*, along with accompanying rallies and a film series, provided a scathing critique of the influences of liberalism and secularism in Western culture. In spite of the popularity of his work, few in my circle of friends were aware of the growing interest among some evangelical leaders in engaging in politics in a much more partisan way to "wage war" against these cultural shifts.

The student ministry in which my faith had flourished and the dispensational seminary within which I had come to understand evangelicalism scarcely mentioned social concern and political activism. Thus, when Jerry Falwell and associates founded the Moral Majority in 1979 and quickly aligned the movement with the Republican Party, I had no idea that the evangelical label by which I defined myself was going to be redefined for decades to come by that burgeoning movement.

My wife and I moved to Eastern Europe in 1982 and did not move back to the United States until 1995. During our time in Europe, the label *evangelical*, as it was understood in the United States, was largely irrelevant to us. In Germanic regions, *evangelische* referred to the historic Lutheran Church. In southern Poland, where we lived for seven years, members of non-Lutheran Protestant churches simply called themselves "believers." Because that region, also known as Silesia, had been a part of Germany for centuries, *evangelical* was still tied to Lutheranism. Because of the historical cultural dominance of Roman Catholicism in Poland, calling yourself "Christian" identified you as Roman Catholic. Interestingly, *believer* was broad enough to work not only in Baptist, Brethren, and Pentecostal circles but also within renewal movements in the Roman Catholic and Lutheran faith communities.

The way we identified ourselves religiously depended on the way the broader community understood those labels. As missionaries, our goal was to identify ourselves with a community in a way that created the least amount of misunderstanding and resistance to the gospel (see 1 Corinthians 9:19-23). I think that same approach to identity and mission is essential for evangelicals in the United States today.

When we came back to the United States in the 1990s, it quickly became clear to us that, with their large media platforms, groups such as Jerry Falwell's Moral Majority, Pat Robertson's 700 Club, and James Dobson's Focus on the Family had created an understanding of *evangelical* that I scarcely recognized. *Evangelical* had morphed from an identity grounded in gospel terms to a movement defined by "culture wars" and partisan political activism. In mass media and the broader cultural landscape, evangelicals were known far more for the ballots they cast than for the beliefs they held. The evangelical identity I had embraced in the seventies was no longer the predominant understanding of the movement.

Although firmly entrenched for the past twenty years in educational institutions that self-identify theologically as evangelical, I have experienced a growing fear that the understanding of evangelicalism in the United States as a partisan political movement has eclipsed the theological and missional identity that remains so dear to me.

And that's why my friend's question, "Why are you an evangelical?" made me pause. I knew she understood *evangelical* as a partisan political identity, an identity she didn't share or agree with. For her and for millions of other Americans, the evangelical label now carries such a negative connotation that it distorts their understanding of the gospel. That reality is a crisis for evangelicals in the United States and a tragedy for those who simply cannot hear the gospel through the din of our partisan political engagement.

A CRISIS OF IDENTITY AND MISSION

Now, thirty-seven years after the 1980 presidential election, when evangelicals began their very public and very partisan political activism, membership in evangelical churches is in decline, and by almost every measure, the social and moral issues for which the culture wars were waged have not moved in the direction evangelicals desired. Evidently what we so smugly thought to be true in 1978 about the negative effect on church growth among liberal Protestants wrought by enthroning political engagement above gospel proclamation is true. We're experiencing it firsthand.

At least liberal Protestantism has retained its cultural power in the face of declining membership. We can't claim that. The fact that the candidate preferred by a strong majority of self-identified evangelical voters sits in the Oval Office should not be confused with any kind of victory in the culture wars or with growing cultural power for evangelicals. Indeed, the opposite is true. More people voted for the candidate in the 2016 presidential election endorsed by mainline Protestant denominations than the candidate supported by evangelicals.

Moreover, on key social issues such as same-sex marriage, abortion rights, premarital sex, cohabitation before marriage, and physician-assisted suicide, trends indicate that fewer Americans are adopting the positions traditionally espoused by conservative evangelicals.[3] After the 2012 presidential election, Al Mohler wrote,

> Millions of American evangelicals are absolutely shocked by not just the presidential election, but by the entire avalanche of results that came in. It's not that our message— we think abortion is wrong, we think same-sex marriage is wrong—didn't get out. It did get out. It's that the entire moral landscape has changed. An increasingly secularized America understands our positions and has rejected them.[4]

The subjugation of evangelicalism's theological identity and missional priority to political partisanship was on full display in the 2016 presidential campaign and election. Although many evangelical leaders have focused on the victories of the candidates they endorsed, the losses suffered by the entire movement are far more significant than any political gains. Our theological identity, our moral integrity, the credibility of our witness, and any progress that we've made in racial reconciliation, relationships with immigrant groups, and international partnerships have all been negatively affected.

It isn't difficult for those outside the movement to note the hypocrisy of evangelicals who excoriated Bill Clinton for his moral failures while being seemingly unconcerned about Donald Trump's personal morality.[5] Thabiti Anyabwile, pastor of Anacostia River Church in Washington, DC, has been quoted as saying, "You've now hitched your wagon to the GOP and Mr. Trump in ways that just ruin moral credibility in the country. . . . I don't know how you recover from that." He went on, "Evangelicals in this vote have created a pretty deadly and chilling effect on their witness to Christ and the gospel and the scriptures. . . . There's not only a credibility problem in terms of the body politic. There's also an evangelistic problem."[6]

It doesn't seem to be hyperbole to assert that evangelicalism is suffering a crisis of identity and mission. The crisis is a self-inflicted wound. It is at its core a theological crisis, but its negative effects are most acute in the area of gospel witness. Whereas most evangelicals still confess allegiance to the core doctrines of biblical authority, eternal salvation based on the atoning work of Christ, and the need for personal piety, our understanding of ecclesiology remains underdeveloped, and therefore our commitment to mission is undervalued. In other words, we don't know *who* we are, and we've lost sight of *why* we are who we are. An anemic theological understanding of the church has contributed to the movement's evolution into a partisan political coalition rather than a gospel-centered presence of the people of God.

Evangelicalism's core theological identity has been remarkably resilient across historical eras, geographical settings, and cultural differences. David Bebbington's Quadrilateral has remained relevant in contemporary American evangelicalism even though the original book specifically addressed the movement's history in Britain over two hundred years ago.[7] The National Association of Evangelicals (NAE), for example, has utilized his four central points "to provide a consistent standard for identification of evangelical belief." They summarize those four points as follows:

- conversionism: the belief that lives need to be transformed through a "born-again" experience and a lifelong process of following Jesus

- activism: the expression and demonstration of the gospel in missionary and social reform efforts

- biblicism: a high regard for and obedience to the Bible as the ultimate authority

- crucicentrism: a stress on the sacrifice of Jesus Christ on the cross as making possible the redemption of humanity[8]

Whether these four theological commitments will define evangelicalism into the future is an open question, but their persistence in defining the movement up to this time is striking. The question that must be answered today, however, is how these four defining beliefs relate to the movement's embrace of partisan political engagement to achieve social and cultural change as its primary identity and mission.

A THEOLOGICAL BLIND SPOT

It is telling that Bebbington's Quadrilateral doesn't include a statement about the church. He rightly observes that evangelicalism per se has not engaged in serious theological reflection on the nature and mission of the church to the degree that it has explored other areas of theology.

Writing as an evangelical, Millard Erickson notes, "At no point in the history of Christian thought has the doctrine of the church received the direct and complete attention which other doctrines have received."[9] Although this is surely overstated when one considers historical Roman Catholic and Eastern Orthodox theologies, Erickson's statement rings true for evangelical theological reflection.

In an aptly titled essay, "Is Evangelical Ecclesiology an Oxymoron?" Bruce Hindmarsh points to evangelicalism's transdenominational character as a primary reason that ecclesiology has not been a high priority in evangelical theology. He writes, "Early modern evangelicalism displayed an unprecedented transdenominational and international ecclesial consciousness that was characterized by an unparalleled subordination of church order to evangelical piety."[10] His observation raises two critical issues that may help us understand some of the dynamics underlying the changing nature and identity of evangelicalism: (1) the limitations of a transdenominational movement and (2) the loss of clarity about the mission of God's people.

The transdenominational character of evangelicalism in the United States contributed to its impressive growth and expanding social power. It has also made evangelicalism notoriously difficult to define and impossible to direct. As a loosely allied coalition of various denominations, churches, academic institutions, media outlets, mission agencies, and popular leaders, evangelicalism befuddles those who want to compare it to established religious entities with recognized authority structures. No single person or organization speaks authoritatively for evangelicals or evangelicalism as a whole. Although the National Association of Evangelicals has a membership that is broadly representative, it exercises no power over its members and is not necessarily considered by the broader culture as an official voice for the movement. Evangelicalism is so different from historically recognized churches and denominations that the broader culture simply does not know how to define it religiously. To many outside the movement, it seems amorphous and chaotic yet somehow powerful and threatening. What, if anything, creates its identity and holds evangelicalism together as a movement?

As with most social movements, evangelicalism may be defined as "an identifiable set of groups and individuals with some common history and traits."[11] In many regards, evangelicalism was the common name for revival movements in England and colonial America in the eighteenth and nineteenth centuries. These revivalist beginnings established evangelicalism's emphasis on personal conversion and piety. That shared experience by thousands of traditional Christians crossed established denominational boundaries.

Early evangelicalism often defined itself as much by what it wasn't as by what it was. Although more fluid than many in the movement would have wished, evangelicalism's boundaries were often drawn in contrast to other religious entities, particularly Roman Catholicism. Antipapist rhetoric flowed freely in evangelical teaching. Its transdenominational character promoted a spiritual autonomy and anti-authoritarianism that mirrored the spirit of the Revolutionary Era.[12] These traits, as a continuation of the Protestant rejection of medieval Roman Catholicism, diminished the role and authority of the church in matters of salvation, spiritual life, and social identity. But Roman Catholicism wasn't the only religious identity that evangelicalism used to create its own identity. In the twentieth century, fundamentalism and liberal Protestantism played equally important roles in demarcating evangelicalism as a religious and social movement.

Evangelicalism and fundamentalism were essentially indistinguishable theologically and sociologically in the late nineteenth and early twentieth centuries in the United States. The nature of the relationship between evangelicalism and fundamentalism is a matter of some scholarly disagreement. However one understands the origins of the two movements, it would be safe to say that most scholars see contemporary evangelicalism, sometimes called neo-evangelicalism, as being shaped by its differentiation from fundamentalism and theological liberalism.[13] This differentiation occurred in the mid-twentieth century when several prominent theologians, pastors, and evangelists promoted the need to distinguish evangelicalism from the decidedly negative caricature of fundamentalism that emerged in the press after the Scopes trial in 1925. But at the same time, these leaders, sometimes called neo-evangelicals, wanted to preserve the movement's emphasis on biblical authority and distance themselves from Protestant theological liberalism.[14]

One cannot understand the tensions in evangelical identity today without carefully considering the movement's kinship with the fundamentalist movement and the causes of the split between the two. Since neither movement has a formal organizational structure, the boundaries between evangelicalism and fundamentalism are often vague, particularly to outsiders. Although many evangelicals today find the fundamentalist label offensive, the movement continues to share theological commitments and many conservative social values with fundamentalism.[15]

Consistent with its polemic against Roman Catholicism and its emphasis on personal conversion, the fundamentalist movement assiduously avoided the creation of ecclesiastical structures and authority outside local congregations. Strong personalities utilized itinerant preaching, print publications, and radio broadcasts to develop widespread, loyal followings. Their popularity gave them significant social and religious power within the movement. These figures took on themselves the authority to control the boundaries of acceptable belief and behavior within fundamentalism. Conservatism and control remain dominant social values in fundamentalism and evangelicalism. Denunciation, social shaming, and ostracism are powerful tactics used to enforce those values.

Biblical literalism and inerrancy were watchwords of the fundamentalist movement. Bibliology, what one believed about the nature of the Bible and how to read it, became the watershed issue for controlling the boundaries of fundamentalism and determining one's standing in the movement. Although one could wholeheartedly agree with fundamentalism's positions on any number of theological issues, if one dared question biblical literalism and inerrancy, the social consequences would likely be severe. Biblical literalism and inerrancy meant that a literal reading of the text was considered normative for all parts of Scripture. Furthermore, it demanded that all biblical texts be read as historically accurate.

The Scopes trial of 1925 created a perfect forum to highlight fundamentalism's insistence that the biblical creation account was to be interpreted literally and taken as historically accurate. This trial put fundamentalism's opposition to modernism, particularly the widespread adoption of Darwinism as an alternative explanation for origins, on public display. Although many within the movement saw the outcome of the trial as a victory, the negative public perception of fundamentalist Christianity as antiscience and anti-intellectual has been firmly entrenched in the wider culture to this day. Evangelicals are still often identified with these characteristics.

The desire to hold onto many of the theological commitments of fundamentalism, while at the same time acknowledging the value of science and other nonsectarian academic disciplines, was one of the central factors in the development of a "new" evangelicalism that has attempted to differentiate itself from early twentieth-century fundamentalism. Resolving the tension between legitimate scholarship and doctrinal compliance was important to evangelical scholars and academics as a way to distinguish themselves from fundamentalists. Vernon Grounds, long-serving president of Denver Seminary, captured well an evangelical approach to the tension with this description of the seminary in the 1965: "Here is no unanchored liberalism—freedom to think without commitment. Here is no encrusted dogmatism—commitment without the freedom to think. Here is vibrant evangelicalism—freedom to think within the bounds laid down in Scripture."[16]

Fundamentalism was also known for its strict codes of conduct, often expressed through an imposing array of prohibitions against various behaviors. Just as the movement valued control and conformity in areas of doctrine, the same was expected in regard to behavior. Although the proscribed behaviors varied somewhat among fundamentalist schools and churches, the lists often contained the following prohibited activities: alcohol consumption, dancing, playing cards, going to movies, immodest dress, and public displays of affection between unmarried men and women. To remain within the movement, one had to abide by strict behavioral guidelines or fear the same consequences as those guilty of doctrinal deviation: denunciation, social shaming, and ostracism.

The evangelicalism that attracted so many of us in the 1960s and '70s presented itself as an alternative to fundamentalism. On the one hand, evangelicalism attempted to break free from the cultural stereotype of fundamentalism as anti-intellectual and antiscience. Evangelical colleges and seminaries strove mightily to develop intellectually credible, accredited educational programs. Christian intellectuals and scholars were afforded significant respect in academic circles and applauded publicly by evangelical leaders. Campus ministries challenged students and graduates to integrate their faith commitments into the academic disciplines and professional fields that they were choosing as careers. On the other hand, evangelical churches, colleges, and seminaries continued to require doctrinal compliance with the fundamental tenets of historic Christian orthodoxy to participate in the community. This compliance was thought to differentiate evangelicalism from the theological liberalism of mainline Protestantism.

In like manner, evangelicalism during this period offered an attractive alternative to the strict behavioral standards of fundamentalism and the perceived antinomianism of theological liberalism. Dramatic changes in cultural norms challenged fundamentalism's instincts to conserve and control. Evangelical churches and ministries, while affirming the need for personal piety, typically offered much stronger overtones of mercy and grace than more legalistic fundamentalist churches and schools.

Evangelical youth and campus ministries welcomed everyone regardless of dress, appearance, and personal hygiene, while fundamentalist schools made compliance with strict codes for dress and personal appearance matters of biblical obedience. Evangelical ministries also adopted popular music forms. When I was a college student in the 1970s, the evangelical campus ministry that reignited my faith offered a wonderfully attractive mix of gospel, worship, teaching, fellowship, and humor.

As a transdenominational movement, evangelicalism and its limited doctrinal core made it possible for a wide variety of individuals, churches, and ministry organizations to consider themselves to be evangelical. Evangelicalism has been an unofficial, and sometimes unwelcome, presence in some mainline churches, at times leading to local churches pulling out of their historically liberal denominations. Although it clearly differentiated itself from the liberal theologies of mainline Protestantism, evangelicalism wanted to be known as a movement that was as intellectually vibrant and conversant with contemporary cultural trends as mainline Protestantism. Fundamentalist churches and denominations have not shared that desire.

Whereas evangelicalism's doctrinal profile created a bright line of differentiation from mainline Protestantism, its separation from fundamentalism began from a place of agreement deeper than any disagreement. With a shared set of foundational beliefs, evangelicalism and fundamentalism have more in common than many evangelicals today will comfortably admit. Evangelicals instinctively lean toward theological and social conservatism. That conservatism creates a negative reaction to cultural and social change that challenges deeply held values from the past. The tumultuous cultural and social upheavals of the 1960s and '70s "shook what many conservative Protestants thought of as the foundations of American society."[17]

For many conservative evangelicals, changes in theological understandings, social patterns, and moral norms threaten the instinct to control. The perceived loss of control then spawns the impulse to fight back. It isn't surprising, therefore, that evangelicals have consistently been politically conservative and frequently frame their engagement in politics with the language of apocalypse, fear, and warfare.

As a transdenominational movement, evangelicalism lacks the theological foundation, organizational structures, and leadership to develop a shared theological understanding of culture, power, social responsibility, politics, and government. In my perspective, the crisis in evangelical identity isn't driven by substantive changes in the core beliefs (think Bebbington's Quadrilateral) that have defined the movement for generations. It is grounded in an inadequate understanding of how those core beliefs ought to shape one's sense of national identity, religious identity, and social responsibility, areas that are directly related to ecclesiology and mission.

As evangelicalism was a transdenominational movement, its traditional approaches to ecclesiology were irrelevant, because they focused on issues that typically created the very denominational divisions that evangelicalism spanned. Therefore, there seems to have been no perceived need to address the glaring omission of ecclesiology in evangelicalism's shared doctrinal core. This theological deficiency has contributed to the movement's embrace of a sociopolitical identity and mission above its theological identity and mission. As stated before, we seem to have forgotten who we are and why we are who we are.

A WAY FORWARD?

A much more apropos and powerful transdenominational ap proach to ecclesiology, one that moves beyond the discipline's traditional focus, is critical for evangelicalism. Such an approach has gained traction in recent years through the language and theology of *missio Dei* and missional church. When used as a hermeneutical and theological paradigm, *missio Dei* has generated vibrant scholarly research and innovative thinking about the identity and mission of the church.[18]

In a missional ecclesiology, the church is understood within the hermeneutical and theological framework of the *missio Dei*, defined as God's intent (transcendent, eternal) and actions (immanent, historical) whereby all peoples may know and worship him. Although missional ecclesiology[19] is still relatively young in its development, some consistent characteristics are beginning to emerge. For example, a missional ecclesiology will often use the phrase "the people of God" as a way to emphasize continuity in the identity and mission of God's people in the Old and New Testaments. Both Israel and the church are called by God to be his particular and peculiar people for the sake of making him known to the nations and to become a means for the blessing of all people. Therefore, in a missional ecclesiology, election is understood as God's act of setting apart a people unto himself, through whom he executes his mission. God's election is not just an election to salvation but also an enlistment to service in God's universal mission of redemption.

In a missional ecclesiology, everything that God does to, for, on behalf of, among, and with his people is to shape them for the mission of making his presence tangible, knowable, and accessible. Mark Lau Branson notes, "God's grace—that is, God's initiatives through Scripture, God's love for the world, God's missional heart, God's great redeeming presence in Jesus Christ—is to be most clearly visible and tangible in faith communities."[20] Therefore, everything the church does must be intentionally designed to support that mission. In other words, the mission of God's people and, therefore, the rationale for everything they do as the church is to establish a tangible, accessible, and life-giving presence of the gospel. It's that magnificently simple and stunningly profound.

Our identity as God's people, those who have experienced redemption and now create a compelling presence and testimony of that redemption, takes precedence over all other identities— racial, social, national, and political. And God's redemptive mission takes precedence over all the church's other activities. A missional ecclesiology subsumes all that we do as God's people, including our engagement in the political process, under the singular purpose of God's redemptive mission in the world.

Partisan politics is a zero-sum game in which one party's gain creates the other party's loss. The people of God, on the other hand, are called to engage others in a way that seeks *their* gain, redemption through Christ, at the expense of personal loss. That's why engagement in partisan politics is inimical to the identity and mission of the people of God. We are called to be the presence of the Christ who died to redeem all people. We are called to be an outpost of the gospel, a community whose primary concern is to make known the God in whom we have the hope of redemption.

Should evangelicals engage in the political process? Of course. A community of the redeemed brings the virtues of the Redeemer into their communities. But participation in the political process must always be undertaken with the goal of enhancing a community's awareness of the Redeemer. Evangelicals must ask themselves the following questions: Did our partisan engagement in the 2016 presidential election make God's loving offer of redemption more compelling to the 65.8 million Americans who voted for the candidate that evangelicals did not support? And has our unwillingness to publicly rebuke candidates and elected officials whom we support politically for their blatant mendacity, demeaning and dehumanizing speech, disregard for the poor and vulnerable, and moral failures commended the gospel to the broader society and compelled belief? It would be difficult to answer either question affirmatively.

The evangelical identity crisis is a self-inflicted wound. We have chosen to make our political identity more important than our gospel identity. And we have chosen to pour our resources and our reputation into a mission of far less importance than the one for which we were created: making the gospel of Jesus Christ a compelling presence in our society. And that is to our shame.

"Why are you an evangelical?"

My friend's question still rings in my ears.

I am an evangelical because I believe that the gospel of Jesus Christ is "good news that will bring great joy to all people" (Luke 2:10 NLT). It's as simple as that. To the degree that evangelicalism continues to define itself by anything other than the gospel, answering my friend's question will remain problematic for those of us who care about how the broader culture hears the gospel. If we are not radically and persistently intentional about defining evangelicalism in the terms of the gospel, I see no reason to continue to use a label that now misrepresents our true identity and is counterproductive to our calling as the people of God's mission. However, if we are willing to refocus our identity and mission on the gospel, we can boldly assert the reason for our identification with evangelicalism. That is my hope and prayer.

4

IMMIGRATION AND THE LATINA/O COMMUNITY

ROBERT CHAO ROMERO

Rosa was a student in my class last year. Toward the end of the term, she asked if I would share with her my lecture slides from the past three classes. She had missed class because her mother had been wrongfully arrested and detained by immigration authorities. Her mom had "papers," but she had been swept up in an immigration raid because she was Latina. My student had returned home to watch her siblings so her father could find her mother. It took four days for them to locate her and rescue her from the wrongful detention. Four days.

A five-alarm fire is raging through the Latino community. Relatively few outside our community—and very few within the evangelical community—seem to care. In fact, through their xenophobic rhetoric, many are intentionally stoking the flames without regard to the many lives being consumed.

Recent executive orders on immigration are spreading terror throughout immigrant communities, and families like Rosa's are being torn apart. Why? Because these executive orders have expanded the definition of "criminal" so broadly that it includes all eleven million undocumented immigrants as targets for deportation. Arrests of immigrants with no criminal records have doubled.[1] Under the previous administration (which was no friend of immigrants, to be sure), perpetrators of serious crimes, at least in theory, were prioritized for deportation. Families and those without criminal records were relegated to the end of the line.

The new immigration enforcement guidelines have led to unconscionable arrests and deportations in recent months, including the detention of a ten-year-old girl with cerebral palsy who had just left the hospital after receiving emergency gall bladder surgery; an undocumented mother who was hospitalized with a brain tumor;[2] an undocumented father who was dropping his child off at school;[3] and a domestic violence victim who was testifying in court.[4]

Pastor Noe Carias's story clearly illustrates how immigrant families are being targeted by the recent executive orders. Noe, an Assemblies of God pastor, has lived in the United States for more than two decades. At the age of eight, during the civil war in Guatemala, he was kidnapped by guerillas. After five years in captivity, he escaped and fled to the United States. Noe eventually married a US citizen and became the father of two beautiful US citizen children. He has no criminal record. And yet, in July he was arrested and detained by Immigration and Customs Enforcement (ICE) during a periodic check-in with immigration officials.

Since Noe's arrest, Deferred Action for Childhood Arrivals (DACA) has also been repealed. This executive action was implemented in 2012 after Congress failed to pass the Dream Act. Undocumented youth were shielded from deportation and granted work permits by DACA. Though DACA was imperfect and was never intended to be a permanent solution, it gave hope to eight hundred thousand undocumented youth who had been brought to the United States as children.

One of my students, Kari, described her faith, her immigration journey, and the opportunities that opened up for her because of DACA.

The dream began with my parents, two young warriors, determined to escape a world of poverty in search for a future in a country where—rumor had it—dreams came true. They sacrificed everything they held dear so I could carry on with their dreams. America has seen me grow, cry, hurt, laugh, and fight for twenty-four years since I migrated at eight months old from Oaxaca. The sobering truth about what it means to be undocumented in this country wounded my validity and identity. The limitations, persecution of undocumented communities, and fear of separation from my family pushed me into coping through art, music, and smoking. I held a great grudge against God for years. But in 2012, I received a wonderful gift in this country—the salvation, grace, and love from Jesus Christ. I realize Jesus brought me to this country as a foreigner to understand vulnerability and marginalization to be more like Him. When I had to pay $5,000 out-of-pocket to attend UCLA because undocumented students didn't get financial aid, He provided. He knew my desire to become an educator and made the way with DACA. Now I stand as a kindergarten and first-grade special education teacher completely in love with serving the children of this community. My identity and citizenship are found in Christ, and no human law will change this. I rest in His love, knowing that He too was despised and rejected but that He loves with an unfailing love. My dream and purpose in this country is to be a fountain of His love and grace.

Like Kari, millions of Latinos in the United States find our identity and citizenship in Christ. In the face of xenophobic rhetoric and hatred, we rest in His love and find comfort knowing that He too was despised and rejected. In this important theological sense, we have been—and remain—evangelical. At the same time, however, many of us feel deeply hurt by the perceived apathy of the evangelical church in response to our suffering. Though we suffer, we don't see the rest of the body of Christ suffering with us (see 1 Corinthians 12:26). For this reason, in an institutional sense, it's difficult for us to identify as evangelicals. Unfortunately, this feeling of institutional and cultural alienation is not new to our recent and historical experience as Latinos in the United States.

THE LATINO THREAT NARRATIVE

For more than a century, the evangelical church in America has been largely complicit in what scholars call the Latino Threat Narrative. According to University of California, Irvine, professor Leo Chávez,

> The Latino Threat Narrative posits that Latinos are not like previous immigrant groups, who ultimately became part of the nation. According to the assumptions and taken-for-granted "truths" inherent in this narrative, Latinos are unwilling or incapable of integrating, of becoming

part of the national community. Rather, they are part of an invading force from south of the border that is bent on reconquering land that was formerly theirs (the US Southwest) and destroying the American way of life.[5]

Mexican Americans were scapegoated for the economic woes of the Great Depression, and between 1930 and 1935, 345,839 Mexicans were repatriated or deported back to Mexico.[6] Tragically, Mexican Americans were not excluded from these deportations. In California, over 80 percent of the repatriates were US citizens or legal residents of the United States. Moreover, between 1947 and 1954 (when my father's family first came to the United States from Mexico), the Immigration and Nationalization Service boasted of apprehending more than one million unauthorized Mexican immigrants as part of the notorious Operation Wetback.[7] Asian Americans, Italians, and Eastern European Jews have also been targets of broader immigrant-threat narratives. Between 1924 and 1965, immigrants from China (my mother's side of the family), Japan, Korea, the Philippines, Italy, Greece, Poland, and Russia were effectively banned from the United States. In fact, between 1790 and 1952, only whites were allowed to become naturalized US citizens.

Motivated by the rhetoric of the Latino Threat Narrative, anti-immigrant federal and state laws have also proliferated over the past two decades. Examples include California Proposition 187 (1994), the federal Sensenbrenner Immigration Bill (2005), Hazleton, Pennsylvania's Illegal Immigration Relief Act (2006), Arizona SB 1070 (2010), Alabama House Bill 56 (2011), and 162 other anti-immigrant laws passed by state legislatures in 2010 and 2011.[8] Capitalizing on the Latino Threat Narrative for political gain, then presidential candidate Donald Trump ran on the xenophobic platform of "Build the Wall" and famously declared, "When Mexico sends its people, they're not sending their best. . . . They're sending people that have lots of problems, and they're bringing those problems with us. They're bringing drugs. They're bringing crime. They're rapists. And some, I assume, are good people."[9]

I assume that most readers of this chapter—regardless of political orientation—are troubled by immigrant threat narratives and the ways in which they have been used to harm marginalized groups. (For the record, I am neither a Republican nor a Democrat, but an "unaffiliated" voter.) And yet I know that 80 percent of self-described evangelicals voted for a president who espouses these views. I also know that the vast majority of evangelicals in the United States have remained silent in the face of the repeal of DACA and the unspeakable arrests and deportations previously mentioned. To be honest, this confuses me. It angers me. It hurts me.

How would you feel if you were in my shoes? Or if you were Kari? Or Pastor Noe? Or Noe's wife and children? Are you not our sisters and brothers in Christ?

As a pastor whose main spiritual gift is evangelism, my heart breaks for another reason as well. It breaks because I know that the current evangelical silence is destroying the reputation of Jesus before a watching world. I see this every day as a professor at the University of California, Los Angeles, and in the academic and activist circles in which I swim. Evangelical silence reinforces the dominant cultural narrative, which says that Christians don't care, that the message of Jesus aligns with xenophobia, and that if we want more racial justice in America, we need less

Christianity. As a result, millions are hindered from coming to know Jesus and the good news he announced and embodied.

LOSING THE NEXT GENERATION

The embrace of the Latino Threat Narrative by some evangelicals has also caused many Latino Christian millennials to walk away from the church. This tragic phenomenon is demonstrated by the story of one of my former students. Carlos grew up in the Southern California and was both a top student and a strong evangelical Christian. His parents were church leaders, and he was active in his church youth group. After graduating from high school, he was accepted to UCLA. Since he was undocumented, however, he didn't know how he was going to afford college. Seeing Carlos's high potential, a generous donor agreed to pay for his first year's educational expenses.

I distinctly remember the first time I met Carlos, because he was carrying an obscure, erudite Spanish translation of the Bible, and he was eager to show it to me. Things soon started to get rough for him during his freshman year, however, when his father was deported. Then his sister was deported and dropped off in Tijuana in the middle of the night by the Border Patrol. Carlos's uncle and cousin had also been deported not too long before that—after calling the police to report a burglary in their home. After Carlos's father was separated from the family, Carlos felt he had no other choice but to use his scholarship money to help support his mother and siblings.

That same year, Carlos visited an evangelical group on campus. Instead of finding support and fellowship, however, he encountered blatant racism. After disclosing to another Christian student that he was undocumented, he was called a criminal.

Feeling ostracized by Christians on campus, he found friends in the Latino activist community. For the first time, he found students who understood his suffering and were active in promoting social change. Although his activist friends were highly supportive, they were not followers of Jesus. In fact, based on their own experience and what they were taught in classes, they believed that Christians were racist and didn't care about the Latino community. Unfortunately, Carlos's negative experience with the Christian group on campus only reinforced this perspective, and he walked away from the evangelical church. That was nearly a decade ago, and he hasn't come back.

THE BIBLICAL PERSPECTIVE

As *evangelicos*, we Latino Christians look to the Bible as the inspired Word of God and the sole infallible rule of faith and practice. Reading our Bibles has taught us that the Latino Threat Narrative is unbiblical and that God's heart yearns for us, his immigrant children. We know that, from beginning to end, the Bible commands the world, and especially God's people, to love immigrants and protect them from mistreatment and injustice. As revealed to Moses, "When an alien resides with you in your land, you shall not oppress the alien. The alien who resides with you shall be to you as the citizen among you; you shall love the alien as yourself, for you were aliens in the land of Egypt: I am the Lord your God" (Leviticus 19:33-34 NRSV). And "cursed is the one who perverts the justice due the stranger [immigrant], the fatherless, and widow" (Deuteronomy 27:19 NKJV).

As we've read our Bibles and reflected on our immigration experiences, we've discovered an important scriptural principle: *Migration is a source of God's grace both to migrants and their host country.*[10] Many of us, as former Catholics, know that grace is not just forgiveness but God's unmerited favor extended to every aspect of our lives. Through the Scriptures and our own migration journeys, we know that God uses the migration process to share His grace with both immigrants and the countries that are privileged to receive them.

Many biblical narratives bear out this spiritual principle. The call of Abraham is a primary example. God affected the salvation of the world through Abraham's obedience in emigrating from Ur. Through Abraham's faithful act of migration and the process it set in motion, all the peoples of the earth have been and are being blessed by him.

Later in the book of Genesis, we encounter Joseph—a forced migrant who was used by God as a source of grace. Joseph was a slave trafficked to Egypt by his jealous brothers. Yet through a series of divine interventions, he rose to the rank of second in Egypt. Through his position, Joseph saved his whole family, Egypt, and Canaan from famine. He stated as much to his brothers: "You intended to harm me [by forcing me to migrate through slave trafficking], but God intended it for good to accomplish what is now being done, the saving of many lives" (Genesis 50:20 NIV).

As we read our Bibles, we also see that hospitality to strangers is modeled biblically not only on an individual basis but also on a systemic, or structural, one. Stated another way, God's grace was extended to immigrants on a structural level through the legal requirements of the Mosaic law.

Structural provision for the basic needs of immigrants is reflected in the gleaning laws and special tithes divinely instituted in the Mosaic law. According to that law, landowners were to leave for the poor the grain along the edges of their fields as well as the fallen remnants left by the harvest: "When you reap the harvest of your land, do not reap to the very edges of your field or gather the gleanings of your harvest. Leave them for the poor and for the foreigner residing among you. I am the Lord your God." (Leviticus 23:22 NIV).

Moreover, every three years, the entire tithe of produce was to be given to the clergy, immigrants, orphans, and widows, "so they can eat in your cities until they are full" (Deuteronomy 26:12 CEB).

Because of their susceptibility to societal discrimination, the Mosaic law also guaranteed what might be labeled civil-rights protections for the immigrant community: "The alien who resides with you shall be to you as the citizen among you; you shall love the alien as yourself, for you were aliens in the land of Egypt." (Leviticus 19:33-34 NRSV).

In striking similarity to modern US constitutional law, the Mosaic law also required equitable treatment between immigrants and native Israelites, and prohibited the application of disparate legal codes for the two groups: "You are to have the same law for the foreigner and the native-born. I am the LORD your God" (Leviticus 24:22 NIV).

These legal requirements bear a striking resemblance to the Equal Protection Clause of the Fourteenth Amendment to the US Constitution and represent one of its earliest historical precursors.

In the New Testament, we meet Jesus—the Palestinian Jew who grew up with the shame of being conceived out of wedlock and who was forced to migrate to Egypt as a child refugee fleeing political violence. In Jesus' most famous story—the parable of the good Samaritan—he upholds a member of a hated racial and ethnic group as an example of what it means to love our neighbor and fulfill God's commands. And in perhaps the most stunning biblical illustration of the principle of migration as grace, Jesus taught that when we welcome the immigrant/stranger, we are welcoming him.

Moreover, when we reject the stranger, we are rejecting Jesus himself. As he stated,

> "Then the King will say to those on his right, 'Come, you who are blessed by my Father; take your inheritance, the kingdom prepared for you since the creation of the world. For I was hungry and you gave me something to eat, I was thirsty and you gave me something to drink, I was a stranger [*xenos*] and you invited me in. . . .
>
> "Then he will say to those on his left, 'Depart from me, you who are cursed, into the eternal fire prepared for the devil and his angels. For I was hungry and you gave me nothing to eat, I was thirsty and you gave me nothing to drink, I was a stranger and you did not invite me in. (Matthew 25:34-35, 41-43 NIV)

In the language of Latino theology, "What human beings reject, God chooses as His very own."[11]

KEEPING THE ECONOMY AFLOAT

In this current historical moment, undocumented immigrants serve as an important source of grace to the United States through their vast economic contributions in the form of labor and taxes. Simply put, they keep the economy afloat by doing the jobs that nobody else wants to do, at a low price that nobody wants to be paid. Our undocumented friends and family members account for 4.3 percent of the US labor force—about 6.3 million workers out of 146 million. They are clustered in construction, agriculture, the service sector, and domestic work, and they contribute more than $420 billion per year to the nation's gross domestic product (GDP). They build and repair our homes, care for our children when we're at work, pick our fruits and vegetables, stitch our favorite pairs of jeans, clean our homes and hotel rooms, bus our tables, and cook the meals at our favorite restaurants. Many of them also clean and maintain our church buildings and facilities.

What's more, our undocumented friends and family saved Social Security. According to Stephen C. Goss, the chief actuary of the Social Security Administration, unauthorized immigrants contributed up to $240 billion to the Social Security trust fund by 2007.[12] If not for these monumental tax contributions, Social Security would have gone belly up in 2009. Our undocumented family members have saved the livelihoods of millions of senior citizens in our country.

Though undocumented immigrants work hard for this country, the existing broken immigration system doesn't officially recognize their labor. Although an estimated eleven million undocumented immigrants supply upward of $420 billion per year to the US GDP and contribute hundreds of billions of dollars more to federal and state coffers through tax contributions, the US government hasn't recognized these contributions by issuing them a proportionate number of work visas. In 2010, for example, the federal government gave out less than five thousand unskilled-worker visas to every country in the world. Even if it wanted to give more, under current law, it's limited to an annual total of ten thousand.[13] Sometimes it's asked, "Why don't undocumented immigrants just 'fix' their immigration status or 'get in line'?" As an immigration lawyer myself, I can say that this is one of the big reasons: there is no line to enter because the US government doesn't recognize their labor and vast economic contribution.

Eleven million undocumented immigrants plus $420 billion in economic contributions to the GDP equals five thousand unskilled-worker visas. This is a mathematics of injustice. Our immigration system is broken, and the numbers don't add up. As long as nothing is done to fix the broken immigration laws of the United States, our mothers, fathers, uncles, aunts, grandparents, sisters, and brothers will continue to be exploited as disposable cheap labor. To make matters worse, just as in decades past, they continue to be scapegoated for the economic woes of the nation for selfish, short-term political gain. Meanwhile, most of the evangelical church stays silent while continuing to benefit from the sweat, tears, and sacrifice of our loved ones.

Fairness—indeed, biblical justice—requires that the US government recognize the manifold economic contributions of our Latino immigrant friends and families by granting them a concomitant number of work visas and/or legal residency status. To refuse to do so is exploitation (see Deuteronomy 10:17-19; Exodus 23:9; Matthew 25:35-40). The failure to provide immigration relief constitutes oppression, for it perpetuates a system in which eleven million immigrants are exploited for their multibillion-dollar economic contributions but denied basic civil and human rights. It is tantamount to slavery—benefiting from the labor of a human being but purposefully denying her or his fundamental humanity.

CONCLUSION

At this critical juncture in US history, we, the evangelical church, are faced with a crucial question: Will we be Jesus' body in this country?

Will we model to Latino immigrants the radical hospitality of Jesus? Will we humble ourselves to recognize the manifold expressions of grace we receive from them and reciprocate this grace through the compassionate reformation of our immigration laws? Will we call our brothers and sisters who are fanning the flames of xenophobic fire back to the Scriptures and to the radical stranger-oriented nature of our faith?

Mother Teresa called people to meet Jesus in the distressing disguise of the poor. Jesus now appears to us in the distressing disguise of eleven million undocumented immigrants and refugees from Mexico, El Salvador, Guatemala, Honduras, China, the Philippines, and Syria, as well as many other countries throughout the world. Like Jesus fleeing from Herod, many of them, especially those from Central America and Syria, are fleeing violence and bloodshed. Many others are fleeing poverty and social displacement caused by the forces of economic globalization and US international economic policy.

Will we make it right by welcoming, with radical hospitality, the millions of immigrant neighbors who now live in our midst? Will we pass compassionate immigration reform that takes seriously the biblical principle of migration as grace? With God's empowerment, will we commit ourselves to doing all that we can to pass the Dream Act?

If we do not, as evangelical Christians, we will continue to lose credibility in the eyes of tens of millions of Latinos in the

United States, and we will destroy our Christian witness in a watching world. Like Carlos, thousands of Latino millennials will continue to leave the evangelical church. We will all have to answer to Jesus for the choices we make.

Still evangelical? Theologically, yes. Institutionally? Despite the deep hurt that I and many other Latinos feel toward the evangelical church, by whatever name, I will continue to fight for the beloved community of Jesus. This is the same end for which Dr. Martin Luther King Jr. and César Chávez strove during the civil rights movement, and this should be our goal today. In the book of Revelation, John offers an inspiring vision of the beloved community, God's children from every tribe, language, tongue, and cultural group:

> After this I looked, and there before me was a great multitude that no one could count, from every nation, tribe, people and language, standing before the throne and before the Lamb. They were wearing white robes and were holding palm branches in their hands. And they cried out in a loud voice:

> "Salvation belongs to our God,
> who sits on the throne,
> and to the Lamb." (Revelation 7:9-10 NIV)

No one is left out, for in Christ, "there is no longer Jew or Greek, there is no longer slave or free, there is no longer male and female; for all of you are one in Christ Jesus. And if you belong to Christ, then you are Abraham's offspring, heirs according to the promise" (Galatians 3:28-29 NRSV).

5

EVANGELICAL FUTURES

SOONG-CHAN RAH

Historians and missiologists alike agree that the era of Western-centric, white Christianity has drawn to a close. Diversity of races, nationalities, ethnicities, languages, and cultures serve as the norm on a global scale for Christianity. Evangelicalism will thrive in the twenty-first century in no small part due to the increase in the number of nonwhite evangelicals. The trajectory of diversity in global Christianity is also evident in American Christianity, which is increasingly less white and composed more and more of people of color.

A projection of the American population at large indicates that "the minority population is expected to increase to the point that they represent the numeric majority between 2040 and 2050."[1] As Stephen Warner states, "We should recognize that the extent of the new religious and racial diversity in the United States is unprecedented but also not forget that most of the new immigrants are Christian."[2] This increasing diversity in American society will challenge assumptions about the decline of American

Christianity. Rather than seeing a collapse, we may be seeing the revival of American Christianity in a vastly different form.

This new form of American Christianity is exemplified by the increasing presence of Asian Americans in evangelical seminaries, increased church-planting efforts in evangelical denominations by Latinos, the replacement of aging white churches with immigrant churches, and an increase in participation in white megachurches by African Americans.[3] As Warner writes, "New immigrants represent not the de-Christianization of American society but the de-Europeanization of American Christianity."[4]

However, the discussion of the future of American evangelicalism often precludes the central role of nonwhite evangelicals; the assumption of a white-dominated evangelicalism remains entrenched. To move toward a future evangelicalism marked by an integrated and healthy diversity, the current captivity of American evangelicalism to a Western, white cultural dominance must be overcome.

Theological inquiry often begins with an existing social imagination. Our ability to imagine and understand the world often shapes our forward projection of the world. When cultural values shape our imagination, we end up with a culturally captive imagination rather than one rooted in Scripture. As I argue in *The Next Evangelicalism*, American Christianity's captivity to Western, white culture generates a theological imagination that falls short of scriptural admonitions.[5] Instead, a dysfunctional theological imagination develops that biases our theology toward Western, white cultural norms. Theology fails to serve its proper function in providing a biblical view of reality. Instead, it has a dysfunctional role in generating a perspective that arises from the dominant culture rather than from the Scriptures.

A healthy prophetic imagination calls God's people to project possibilities for the church and God's people that more fully capture the whole testimony and witness of Scripture. A dysfunctional imagination results in a view of both Scripture and the world that is culturally captive. In order to challenge the dysfunctional imagination among evangelicals, the whole cannon of Scripture must be addressed. In this chapter, I argue that a new prophetic imagination rooted in the lost biblical practice of lament must emerge in order for us to embrace the next phase of evangelicalism.[6]

THE PROBLEM OF AMERICAN EVANGELICAL EXCEPTIONALISM

A recent mailing from a US-based Christian charity featured a fundraising campaign titled "The poor will not always be with us." The main thrust of the campaign was to challenge the US evangelical church to take seriously a new interpretation of Jesus' words and seek to end extreme poverty within this generation. While the goal is worth seeking, the problematic aspect of the campaign was the subliminal message (particularly given the target audience) that the US evangelical church was responsible to bring about this change. So poverty becomes another problem to solve using American ingenuity and gumption. This material exemplifies the self-perception of exceptionalism in the American church, whose standing as the savior of the world is assumed and goes unchallenged.

American Christian exceptionalism assumes the primacy and supremacy of American Christianity over and against other expressions of Christianity. John Wilsey notes that "the idea that America is a unique nation—an exceptional nation—set apart and qualitatively different from, even superior to, the rest of the world is alive and well."[7] The belief in the exceptional qualities of an American nation superior to other nations finds expression in the church as well. American Christianity asserts itself in the unique position of an exceptional form of Christianity, set apart and even superior to other expressions of Christianity in the world. And American exceptionalism finds its roots in the theological dysfunction of American Christian exceptionalism.

American Christian exceptionalism contributes to a triumphalism that focuses on a narrative of success and victory. When suffering occurs, it's considered a hindrance to the work of God in the world. The narratives of suffering communities, therefore, are considered to be inferior and are ignored or removed from the dominant narrative of triumph. Stories of successful church plants and growing megachurches with huge budgets are front and center in how we tell the story of American evangelicalism. Evangelical conferences must bring in big-name speakers, usually young, hip, white pastors, entrepreneurs, and "thought leaders." These trends perpetuate the triumphalist and exceptionalist narrative of US evangelicalism.

A narrative of success propels white evangelicalism over and above other forms of American Christianity. Spanish-speaking storefront churches embody a profound, faithful spirituality in the midst of suffering. However, for many white evangelicals looking for the next magic formula to grow their churches, these churches may be deemed too small and even "illegal." Many Korean American immigrants gather at five every morning to pray at their church before embarking on a twelve-hour workday. But this expression of spirituality may be ignored among the latest evangelical church fads, because it is spoken in a foreign language or in English with an accent. Native American Christian communities that offer spiritual rituals to the heart of disenfranchised Natives are perceived to have exotic pagan practices that are syncretistic and are inferior to the rich tradition of services such as those of Taizé. African American evangelicalism is considered an inferior brand of evangelicalism, with its emphasis on justice and race issues discounting its leaders from key positions of leadership. Nonwhite expressions of US evangelicalism, therefore, are often portrayed as inferior to the successful formula for ministry put forth by many white evangelicals in mainstream US Christian culture.

The mediating narrative of American evangelical exceptionalism and triumphalism emerges from the dysfunctional imagination of white supremacy. For several decades, white evangelicalism has served as a model of success. Evangelical churches have grown in number and size; they have shaped the spiritual well-being of and given purpose to countless individuals; and they have even influenced and determined elections. This sustains an assumption that this apparent success and triumph by the American evangelical church should cause it to grow unabated. If not, then everything must be done to preserve the power that elevates evangelical exceptionalism. White evangelicals, therefore, have been willing to overlook numerous problems with "their" candidates as long as they supported the white evangelical agenda, even if they were supremely unqualified as well as immoral.

Self-perceived exceptionalism coupled with an unholy pursuit of triumphalism emerges from a dysfunctional theological imagination among US evangelicals that perpetuates an increasingly dysfunctional religion in a diverse world. Despite this profound dysfunction rooted in a diseased theological imagination, white American evangelicalism clings to the assumption that its worldview and cultural engagement is the appropriate and non-negotiable one.

THE LINE OF ORTHODOXY

Evangelicals perceive themselves to be in the line of orthodoxy that traces back to biblical times. They are the inheritors of orthodox Christianity from the chosen line evident in Genesis (Adam, Abel, Seth, Enoch, Noah, Abraham, Isaac, and Jacob) to the chosen nation of Israel (Moses, Joshua, David, and the faithful prophets), to the new covenant community (the New Testament church) birthed in Acts 2, to the missionary efforts of the apostle Paul, to the early church and their martyrs, to the empowered missionary activist church that succeeds the early church, to the faithful remnant in the context of the Roman captivity of the church, to the great Protestant Reformers proclaiming *sola fide* and *sola Scriptura*, to those who seek a pure faith on the canvas of tabula rasa, to the chosen people seeking to establish a city set on a hill, to the experiencers of great revivals (exemplified by Whitefield, Edwards, and Spurgeon, and extending to Wesley and Finney), to the great missionaries of the great mission century, to the great evangelists calling for personal conversion (such as Billy Graham), to the faithful remnant that serve as culture warriors in the midst of the collapse of Christendom.

Evangelicalism transcends denominations, integrating the Lutheran, Presbyterian, and Reformed churches that trace their heritage to the Protestant Reformation; the passion of the Pietists, Puritans, and the Pentecostals; the mission emphasis of the

Moravians and the Methodists; and the zeal of those who claim to seek guidance from the Bible only, such as the Baptists and the Brethren. The various names, threads, and expressions are not as critical as the staunch belief that evangelicals have historically toed the line of orthodoxy. Evangelicals have viewed themselves in that line of orthodoxy in order to justify the framing of evangelical theology through the lens of a bounded set of beliefs and doctrines. Evangelicals, therefore, consistently read the framework of their faith back into the history of Christian orthodoxy as the inheritors and protectors of orthodoxy.[8]

By viewing themselves to be in the line of orthodoxy, US evangelicals face the strong temptation to assume that they inherited a complete and immutable theology. The goal of evangelical theology, therefore, could be seen as the preservation and conservation of received doctrine, rather than a healthy engagement with social-cultural reality. This assumption could lead to a form of cultural captivity as evangelical theology becomes more beholden to a culturally framed theology drawn from a particular context rather than from actual engagement with Scripture and with the person and work of Jesus. In other words, even if the ecclesial practices and the practical applications of American evangelical theology were appropriate for a specific culture and time, we can't assume that these practices should be preserved at all costs, because their context has changed dramatically. The hard boundaries around American evangelicalism don't bode well in a diverse environment.

Evangelicalism in the United States values the boundaries that have been drawn to contain its orthodoxy. Missiologist Paul Hiebert distinguished between two different approaches to the Christian gospel: the bounded set and the centered set. Evangelical theology often operates with bounded-set assumptions that assert the importance of doctrinal boundaries in determining insider and outsider status in the Christian faith. Certain doctrinal positions provide hard boundaries for evangelicals.[9]

The formation of evangelical theology relies on the ability of the white Western mind to produce a rational, Christian worldview that generates authoritative theological boundaries. This bounded set serves as impenetrable doctrine that doesn't allow for the introduction of other perspectives. Other perspectives emerging from other experiences and other cultures are deemed inferior to the bounded-set theology of white evangelicalism. The white evangelical theological worldview, therefore, is elevated to a position of authority on level with the Word of God. And it becomes the defining perspective.

For example, the Western world doesn't experience suffering in ways experienced by the non-Western world. The absence of suffering in the West leads to obsessive inquiry about the reason Jesus suffered on the cross. Volumes have been written in order to grapple with the concept of a suffering Messiah. Outside the comfort of Western culture, Christians readily embrace the suffering Messiah, since his suffering reflects the suffering reality of their world. Others (for example, Latin American theologians) express a desire to engage the Jesus of liberation. Both emphases emerge from a social-cultural experience. However, the emphasis on Jesus crucified is considered more orthodox, while a desire to learn about the liberating power of the gospel is diminished. God expresses his revelation to the whole of humanity, but the authority to speak on the character of God may be diminished because those outside the Western academic world do not share the same social reality or boundary.

Over the last few decades, American evangelicalism has asserted the necessity of a Christian worldview. The evangelical icon Francis Schaeffer provided intellectual fodder in the latter third of the twentieth century. From his perch at L'Abri Fellowship in Switzerland, Schaeffer began to postulate a narrative of the decline of American society. His work tells of a Christian worldview that was under attack in secular American culture. He asserted that, in the past, Christianity had depended on society affirming a Christian worldview, but the presuppositions endemic in secular humanism enabled it to operate as a surrogate religion. This reality necessitated the assertion of a Christian worldview.

While lacking formal education and depth in his analysis, Schaeffer exerted considerable influence on American evangelicalism as one of its key thought leaders. His lectures at Christian colleges made sweeping generalizations about American society that led to apocalyptic conclusions while stirring the hearts of evangelicals who were troubled by the crumbling of a Christendom they believed had existed at one point in American history. Schaeffer's lectures and movies provided the intellectual fodder (as inadequate as it was) for the evangelical masses.

Because the world had fallen captive to secular humanism, evangelicals needed to hang on to a God-honoring worldview, which they believed was rapidly slipping away. Instead of challenging Christendom in the American context, American evangelicals have doubled down on the assumptions of exceptionalism and triumphalism.

The Christian worldview that would come under the control of social, cultural, and political factors would serve as the bounded set for evangelicals. They would not include an orthodox view of Scripture and Christology but would now dictate the need for religious freedoms, prayer in schools, opposition to same-sex marriage, and conservative social and political values. The Christian worldview emerging from the Western mind would provide an impenetrable and superior boundary to those from other cultural settings.

The assumption of the exceptional Western, white Christian worldview would lead to the assumption of a triumphant evangelical theology. In a continuous self-validation loop, triumphalism feeds exceptionalism and excludes any alternative. Since this loop critiques itself, it's not surprising to observe the problematic absence of lament in American evangelicalism. Revealingly, this is a distortion of the very gospel that evangelicalism claims to believe and affirm.

NO ROOM FOR LAMENT

As I previously outlined in *Prophetic Lament*, American evangelicalism has forsaken the spiritual practice of lament. Old Testament scholar Claus Westermann asserts that praise and lament "determine the nature of all speaking to God."[10] Also "laments are prayers of petition arising out of need. But lament is not simply the presentation of a list of complaints, nor merely the expression of sadness over difficult circumstances. Lament in the Bible is a liturgical response to the reality of suffering and engages God in the context of pain and trouble."[11]

Unfortunately, lament is often missing from US evangelical church life. It is skipped over in Scripture readings, in preaching rotations, and in liturgy. The book of Psalms—40 percent of which can be categorized as laments—reveals how lament served as a critical worship practice for God's people. The circumstances of suffering and pain experienced by the people of God required a response of lament.

Lament is the language of suffering. Lament demands humility before God. God's people express their dependence on God in the midst of their distress. Captive to a self-perceived exceptionalism, evangelicalism won't allow for the full expression of pain and suffering that could counteract the assumption of exceptionalism. Narratives that arose from places of suffering can find no place in the metanarrative of evangelical triumphalism.

One example of the counterproductive impact of the narrative of evangelical exceptionalism is the inability to address communities steeped in the experience of lament with anything other than the experience of praise. The narrative of African American Christianity, which emerges from the context of suffering and lament, has often been ignored in mainstream evangelicalism. African American expressions of Christianity hold theologically conservative convictions that mirror evangelical theology, and African American churches contain a spirituality reflective of evangelical theological convictions. Despite these parallels, lament hasn't been accepted into the larger evangelical movement.

As Oberlin College church historian A. G. Miller notes, "Most scholars who study the evangelical phenomenon have had a difficult time situating black Evangelicalism historiographically and tracing its development as a movement."[12] Evangelicalism typically doesn't claim black churches and leaders who have been warriors of social justice and racial equality as their own. The narrative of lament that emerges from the oppression of the African American community is unaccounted for in the history of American evangelicalism.

For example, through my evangelical seminary education, I was taught that Adoniram Judson was the first missionary from the American continent and that William Carey was the first Western missionary. Both individuals have numerous memorials and honors bestowed on them. Judson had a press and a college named after him. Carey had a press and a mission society named after him. However, both of these individuals were preceded by several decades as the first missionary from the West. "George Liele [was] a former slave who left the American colonies for Jamaica in 1782 and began a ministry of preaching in 1783, nearly three full decades before Judson would sail to Burma from Salem, Massachusetts, in 1812 and a full decade before William Carey sailed for India from England."[13]

Liele was a prolific evangelist and church planter in Jamaica. However, despite his pioneering work, he is buried in an unmarked grave. Despite his Baptist ordination, there are no publishing companies, colleges, or even mission agencies named after him. Despite his record of evangelism and church planting, his narrative of lament as a former slave has found no space in the exceptionalism narrative of white American evangelicalism.

In the 1960s and 1970s, when the current expression of American evangelicalism began to take form, a significant group of African Americans identified with the theological and ecclesial sensibilities of this renewal movement. However, over several decades, African American evangelicals were denied leadership in numerous evangelical contexts and were even denied identity as evangelicals. The NBEA (National Black Evangelical Association) would be considered as an ancillary, almost unnecessary organization in comparison to the overwhelmingly white NAE (National Association of Evangelicals).[14]

Even when African American evangelicals adhered to the bounded-set expectations of the larger evangelical movement, they did not find acceptance. They graduated from evangelical institutions such as Wheaton, Moody, Gordon-Conwell, and Fuller Seminary. They worked for evangelical organizations such as InterVarsity, Young Life, and the Billy Graham Evangelistic Association. They would toe the line for every theological non-negotiable put forth by the evangelical theological vanguard. Even with every credential needed to earn the metaphorical evangelical card, few African Americans found acceptance in the evangelical mainstream.

Tom Skinner served as an iconic representative of the movement of black evangelicals in the 1960s and 1970s. A former gang leader, Skinner experienced a dramatic evangelical conversion through an evangelistic radio program. He forsook his violent life and became a prolific evangelist in his late teens. Skinner was recognized as a powerful speaker whose evangelistic appeals called many to faith. The nascent American evangelical movement initially embraced him.

His dramatic conversion story served as a dynamic testimony to the evangelical narrative of an exceptional individual who experienced a conversion in line with evangelical theology. During the 1960s and 1970s, however, Skinner directly addressed the problem of the long history of racial injustice in evangelicalism. In prominent evangelical venues, such as Moody Radio, Wheaton College chapel, and the Urbana mission conferences, Skinner challenged the American evangelical church as he lamented the broken history of race relations in America.

Skinner's presentation of a gospel, which included lament regarding the African American experience, wouldn't find acceptance in American evangelicalism. His Moody Radio program was canceled, and the Christian colleges that had embraced his conversion testimony wouldn't invite him as he began to speak more on racial issues. Contributions to his ministry tapered off. He would be deemed too political, and his message would be seen as straying from a focus on the individual gospel. In short, his message of lament did not jibe with the triumphalism developing among American evangelicals who believed themselves to be the exceptional Christians who were to uphold the bounded set of an individual-focused gospel.

In the African American Christian experience, the painful history of the transatlantic slave trade, the Middle Passage, the oppressive life of slavery on plantations, the backlash against Reconstruction, and suffering under Jim Crow laws provided a narrative of lament. Lament is a primary expression of the African American church experience because pain and suffering are a part of the narrative history of the black church. However, American evangelical exceptionalism and triumphalism would prevent the healthy engagement in and the inclusion of this lament.

A MULTIETHNIC FUTURE

American society and American evangelicalism face a dynamic multiethnic present and future reality. This multiethnic future requires the intersection of praise and lament. The triumphalism of American evangelicalism is an inadequate substitute for the full expression of worship, which includes lament. The future of American evangelicalism must not seek the greatness of American society or the empire of the United States, but must instead seek first the kingdom of God. The fullness of the kingdom of God must include narratives that emerge from lament, not only from praise.

The demographic diversity of American society is a foregone conclusion. The concomitant diversity of American evangelicalism may be upon us faster than the diversification of the American population. Developments in the early part of the twenty-first century, however, have caused many evangelicals of color to reconsider their affiliation with the label of evangelicalism. Although they adhere to the doctrinal values and priorities of evangelicalism, the social, cultural, and political captivity of American evangelicalism to American exceptionalism and triumphalism has caused many to rethink their role in the movement.

Similar to the experience of black evangelicals in the 1960s and 1970s, evangelicals of color in the twenty-first century have jumped through multiple hoops to attain their metaphorical evangelical card. We have attended evangelical colleges and evangelical seminaries. We have served in evangelical ministries, churches, and denominations. If there were an evangelical theological entrance exam, we would pass with flying colors.

However, when it came time to publicly express support for evangelicals of color who were deeply troubled by the rhetoric in our public sphere, our concerns were ignored. When we expressed dismay that black, brown, and yellow bodies would be treated with disdain and contempt, most of our white evangelical brothers and sisters ignored our pleas and added more bricks to the dividing walls of hostility. Yes, the laments of evangelicals of color have been ignored for the sake of white American exceptionalism and triumphalism.

If evangelicals of color were to depart the larger evangelical movement—leaving it with only a shrinking population of white evangelicals—it would not be for impulsive, prideful reasons. It would be a result of white evangelicals creating a hostile environment for evangelicals of color. It would be a result of white evangelicals so caught up in the cultural assumptions of exceptionalism and triumphalism that they are unable to hear the lament of their brothers and sisters.

6

THEOLOGY AND ORTHOPRAXIS IN GLOBAL EVANGELICALISM

ALLEN YEH

The word *evangelical* has come to a critical juncture in Western history, largely due to two momentous events: the 2016 election of Donald Trump as president of the United States of America and the 2017 celebration of the five-hundredth anniversary of the Protestant Reformation. The former has put evangelicals in the political limelight, while the latter gives historicity to evangelicalism. However, both of these are Western definitions: one from the United States and the other from Europe. If *evangelical* comes from *euangelion* (the gospel), and *evangelism* is derived from the same root, then a third consideration is needed: the global interface of evangelicalism and how the Majority World understands and impacts it and is impacted by it. My argument is twofold: the West needs to balance its orthodoxy with orthopraxis, and the Majority World needs to increase its theological output to come into its own.

The question of defining the word *evangelical* is not a new one by any means. My first (coauthored) book was entirely devoted to this subject,[1] and people such as Mark Noll, D. A. Carson, and Roger Olson have penned many volumes on this topic as well. But the US election and the anniversary of the Reformation require that we take a fresh look at *evangelical*, especially with regard to how the word is received today. It also begs us to ask about the utility and meaning of *evangelical*.

ORTHOPRAXIS AS A NECESSARY BALANCE TO WESTERN EVANGELICAL ORTHODOXY

David Bebbington, professor of church history at the University of Stirling in Scotland, gave a historical definition of what an evangelical is: basically any Protestant who affirms the Bebbington Quadrilateral of biblicism, crucicentrism, conversionism, and activism.[2] This was eighteenth- and nineteenth-century evangelicalism, in which people such as John Wesley, Charles Finney, and William Wilberforce exemplified the best of holistic mission; consider the James 1:27 injunction, "Religion that is pure and undefiled before God the Father is this: to visit orphans and widows in their affliction, and to keep oneself unstained from the world" (ESV). Compare that with Wilberforce's mantra, "God Almighty has set before me two great objects: the suppression of the slave trade and the reformation of manners [morals]."[3]

While I agree that the Bebbington Quadrilateral includes four of the hallmarks of evangelicalism, I think one that John Wesley added is necessary: the affections (what we call emotions, evoking a personal relationship with Jesus). His "heart strangely warmed" is the most famous phrase referring to this phenomenon. Another of Wesley's Great Awakening counterparts, Jonathan Edwards (often called "America's greatest theologian"), famously wrote a book called *Religious Affections*, indicating how central this was to the American evangelical identity. So perhaps the quadrilateral should actually be a pentagon.

Despite this historical five-pronged approach, which seems to offer equal emphases on head, heart, and hands, evangelicals in the West today seem to be preoccupied with theological orthodoxy, which is an odd development. In one sense, it's understandable: if Protestantism (the forerunner to evangelicalism) was about faith as opposed to the Catholic tendency toward works, it makes sense that the preached Word should be paramount. Westerners tend to resonate more with the Pauline epistles than, say, the Old Testament prophets. Likewise, Greek systems of thought (historically a later development within Christianity) have influenced Western evangelicalism more than Semitic (Eastern) thought, which is actually the root of the faith.

Platonic thought elevated the spiritual over the material, and this influence has come down to the Western church via theologians such as St. Augustine of Hippo and is still pervasive today. Cartesian philosophy ("I think, therefore I am") and the Enlightenment further contributed to this Western mind/body dichotomy in the seventeenth century, and "the dualities of *savage/civilized* and *body/mind* became paired and reified in the higher education context. Uncovering these histories is important because they are largely invisible to many of us, operating at an unconscious level."[4] Some recent pushback against this tendency is one of the bases for N. T. Wright's "New Perspective on Paul" (setting aside for a moment whether one agrees with it), which argues for a return to Semitic rather than Greek thought, desiring to restore prominence to "doing" rather than only "believing." In a sense, Wright is trying to out-reform the Reformers by going even further back to the cultural milieu of the founders of the faith, and trying to vindicate first-century Jews from having the charge of sixteenth-century Roman Catholic works-righteousness mapped onto them.[5]

This is odd because it doesn't follow historic eighteenth- and nineteenth-century evangelicalism, nor can it claim to be a "back to the Bible" movement, because a Jesus/Semitic kind of Christianity considers that what one does—not just how one thinks—matters. In fact, action may be even more important. The parable of the sheep and the goats (Matthew 25:31-46) is a prime example of this: there is no mention of verbal confession whatsoever; the "sheep" (the ones who go to heaven) are distinguished from the "goats" (the ones who go to hell) by what they do, whether they fed the hungry, gave drink to the thirsty, showed hospitality to the stranger, clothed the naked, looked after the sick, and visited the prisoner.

Although it's true that "everyone who calls on the name of the LORD will be saved" (Romans 10:13 NLT), it is perhaps equally true that "not everyone who says to Me, 'Lord, Lord,' will enter the kingdom of heaven, but only the one who does the will of my Father who is in heaven" (Matthew 7:21). Jesus cursed the fig tree because it did not bear fruit (Matthew 21:18-21; Mark 11:12-14). And the parable of the two sons (Matthew 21:28-32) vindicates the one who did rightly (orthopraxis) even though he didn't say the right thing. The other proclaimed rightly (orthodoxy) though he didn't do the right thing.

The meaning of the parable is clear: the tax collectors and prostitutes who turned to Christ were put before the Pharisees, who had a veneer of righteousness. But somehow this becomes lost on American evangelicals, where the resemblance is more often akin to the Pharisees (they say the right things but are hard in their hearts toward those who are marginalized) than to the marginalized.

Steve Kang incisively points out, "[Missiologist Lesslie] Newbigin is convinced that the West can be converted only by a complete transformation of its mind—away from the distinctive patterns of Enlightenment thought and toward openness to grace, faith, and revelation. He argues that the notion of certainty has been the controlling myth of modernity."[6] Poet-singer-songwriter Rich Mullins said it more colloquially: "If we were given the Scriptures it was not so that we can prove we were right about everything. If we were given the Scriptures it was to humble us into realizing that God is right and the rest of us are just guessing."[7]

Christians do a lot of trying to figure out what Scripture actually says, but we sometimes come up with wildly different interpretations. But would we Protestants say that Catholics and Orthodox are not Christians? I would say that though I disagree with their theology, they are still Christians. So this begs a question: if there are such major differences in theology, and all of these people can still be called Christians, clearly the role of orthodoxy is not the sole determining factor in whether or not you are a Christian. So, what is the point of orthodoxy?

Paul Hiebert, a missiologist from Trinity Evangelical Divinity School, posed this question in an article called "The Category *Christian* in the Mission Task."[8] He posited a situation of a man in India (named Papayya) who hears the gospel from a Western missionary and accepts Jesus as his Lord and Savior. How much does the Indian know about Christianity at this point? Not much, if we're honest. Yet would we say that he's going to heaven? I think most Christians would say yes.

But Papayya probably can't articulate *sola fide* (though he may be living it); he can't talk about the inerrancy of the Bible (in fact, I don't even know whether such a Western modernist categorization would make sense to him); he can't explain the Trinity (but then again, how many Western Christians do you know who can?); he hasn't read much of the Bible (in fact, he might not have read any of it yet); and he probably hadn't ever heard the name of Jesus before several days ago. Yet we call him a Christian and say that he's saved. So again, where does orthodoxy fit in?

Now, what happens if Papayya is wrong about something later in his life? As he reads the Bible and applies it to his context and hears from other preachers, maybe he starts believing something that Western evangelicals wouldn't agree with. In fact, what if it's something we believe to be "heretical"? Would Papayya no longer be going to heaven? Then again, from a Protestant evangelical perspective, why would Papayya be any different from a Catholic as far as we're concerned? And where do you draw the line—a Catholic is a Christian, but a Nestorian is not?

So how much do you have to "know" to be a Christian? And how "right" does it have to be? I'm wondering whether, several centuries from now, people will look back at American Protestant evangelicalism and say, "Wow, they sure got such-and-such wrong." How do we know that we have everything 100 percent correct? Don't you think that God will give us some grace for the things we believed wrongly but sincerely? I sure hope so. And if that applies to us, why shouldn't it apply to

Catholics, Nestorians, Orthodox, Pentecostals? After all, nobody ever acts on what they believe is wrong; everyone always acts on what they believe is right.

Please don't misunderstand me. I am in no way advocating relativism. I believe that there is Truth out there. The only thing that concerns me is that I don't think we can see that Truth in its entirety. We can see only a sliver of it, and we grasp at it sincerely, but sometimes we don't get it right. Neither I, nor you, nor anybody else in this world has assurance that we have got it all right. Nevertheless, I don't think this means we shouldn't try. So we live in this awkward tension between recognizing our fallibility and the fact that right now we only "see through a glass, darkly" (1 Corinthians 13:12 KJV), and we see the need to adhere to truth, because otherwise we become without foundation in what we believe and stand for. Perhaps this is why the apostle Paul calls us to have love with our truth; otherwise we are just resounding gongs or clanging cymbals.

How did we get to this point, where the definition of a Christian is whether or not one is able to check off a list of propositional truths? I suspect that it's a lack of thought in distinguishing between works *before* faith and works *after* faith. While the Protestant Reformers were certainly trying to push back against works-righteousness, many Protestants and evangelicals today mistakenly think that therefore *no* works matter. The truth is, works *after* faith are essential. This is most clearly exemplified by one of the most famous *sola fide* passages, Ephesians 2:8-9: "For by grace you have been saved through faith, and this is not your own doing; it is the gift of God—not a result of works, so that no one may boast" (NRSV). It's followed by verse 10: "For we are His workmanship, created in Christ

Jesus for good works, which God prepared beforehand that we should walk in them" (NKJV).

Let me be clear: this is not to suggest that orthodoxy ought to be dispensed with. This is, rather, a call to reestablish a holistic balance within Western evangelicalism as it has leaned far too heavily on intellectual assent in the twentieth and twenty-first centuries. The reason for a focus on orthopraxis is not that it is preeminent over orthodoxy. However, if a Christian has right action, surely that is a reflection of that person's right thinking. But if he has right thinking, it doesn't mean he necessarily has right action. It is amazing how Jesus' lesson of loving the repentant sinner more than the hardened Pharisee has still not gotten through to so many Western evangelicals who act much more like the latter than the former. And Paul's injunction that truth without love is nothing (1 Corinthians 13:1-2) is another indictment of people who elevate thought over action.

Evangelical Christianity has a PR problem. This is concerning because our name implies that we are to be winsome to draw others in (*evangelical* and *evangelism* share the same root word). David Kinnamon of the Barna Group surveyed non-Christians' perception of Christianity, and he discovered that they think evangelicals are judgmental, hypocritical, antihomosexual, too political, and sheltered.[9] But right action, done winsomely and in a positive, eye-opening way, can help immeasurably.

Right action looks like this: protecting our borders. While this is important, it is the normal tendency of human beings and makes us no different from the world. But to be counterculturally, radically Christian, we have to love the sojourner/stranger/alien/foreigner as ourselves. Leith Anderson, president of the National Association of Evangelicals, points out that this is the third greatest "love" command in the Old Testament after "love God" and "love neighbor."[10] This kind of behavior makes the world sit up and take notice. It doesn't mean we can't protect our own. (Self-preservation and love of the immigrant can coexist.) But as Christians, we *lead off* by considering others before ourselves.

Right action also means amazing love over judgment. When white supremacist Dylann Roof walked into Emanuel African Methodist Episcopal Church in Charleston, South Carolina, on June 17, 2015, and was welcomed to a Bible study with the congregants, he opened fire and massacred nine of them, attempting to incite a race war. When he was arrested and brought to trial, the surviving church members publicly *forgave* him. This kind of behavior makes the world sit up and take notice. They still invited him to repent, but they put forgiveness first. It doesn't mean that sin is inconsequential; love and truth can coexist, but we *lead off* with love.

Right action is often also holistic rather than polarized. While we protect the life of the unborn, we also protect the life of the born (we need to be pro-life "from the womb to the tomb"). Ron Sider, founder of Evangelicals for Social Action, puts it well:

> We must be pro-life and pro-poor, pro-family and pro-creation care, pro-racial justice and pro-peacemaking. This "completely prolife" agenda is now the official stance of both the Catholic bishops and the National Association of Evangelicals.... ESA believes in a "completely pro-life" agenda— i.e., life does not begin at conception and end at birth. When millions die of starvation or diseases we know how to prevent, when millions die prematurely from smoking, when terrorism and war destroy innocent persons, the sanctity of

human life is violated. But that broader "completely pro-life" agenda does not mean we forget about abortion.[11]

Right action means that we do not align ourselves wholly with any one secular social movement. While there are some aspects of the Republican Party that cohere with Christianity, there are some that do not. While there are some aspects of the Black Lives Matter movement that align with Christianity, there are some that do not. We can't count on any one human movement to represent the totality of how Christians should respond; otherwise, what need is there of the church? Christians such as Billy Graham, Martin Luther King Jr., and Mother Teresa have made the world sit up and take notice. They have made history in the best possible way by being prophetic and peaceful. This doesn't mean we can't stand up for justice, but we *lead off* with hope and reconciliation— being a Martin Luther King rather than being a Malcolm X.

This is where the disconnect happens with Majority World[12] evangelicalism, where right thinking is not the most prized expression of the faith. Philip Jenkins describes it:

> These newer churches preach deep personal faith and communal orthodoxy, mysticism and Puritanism, all founded on clear scriptural authority. They preach messages that, to a Westerner, appear simplistically charismatic, visionary, and apocalyptic. In this thought-world, prophecy is an everyday reality, while faith-healing, exorcism, and dream-visions are all basic components of religious sensibility. For better or worse, the dominant churches of the future could have much in common with those of medieval or early modern European times. On present evidence, a Southernized Christian future should be distinctly conservative.[13]

Or perhaps it isn't just a commonality with premodern Europe; it is a commonality with the colonial United States.

Mark Noll, in his book *The New Shape of World Christianity*, argues,

> In recent decades world Christian movements, especially Protestant and independent movements, have come increasingly to take on some of the characteristics of American Christianity. Yet the primary reason for that development is not the direct influence of American Christians themselves. It is rather that social circumstances in many places of the world are being transformed in patterns that resemble in crucial ways what North American believers had earlier experienced in the history of the United States (and to a slightly lesser extent in Canada). Without discounting the importance of direct American involvement around the world, the appearance of Christianities similar to forms of American Christianity highlights parallel development rather than direct influence.[14]

In other words, the thesis of his book is that Christianities in non-Western contexts are going through the same birth, growth, and development stages that US Protestantism already went through some two centuries earlier. It's certainly appreciated that Noll isn't trying to sound paternalistic by implying that the rest of the world merely follows or copies the United States; rather, they are going through a natural process that all nascent Christian revival movements go through.

Majority-World Christians have no problem understanding the necessity of right action, much as the early Christians did. They aren't arguing about Calvinism versus Arminianism or premillennialism versus postmillennialism; they are just trying to follow Jesus. It seems that early Christian movements had a purity about them, but they start to stray or become imbalanced over time as accretions accumulate from human error, misguided traditions, or culture that gets confused with Christianity. Therefore, it's necessary to have periodic reformations to restore balance.

Yet going back to the roots is not always the answer. Moving forward with progressive revelation is required, too, as time passes and new situations arise. Even Pauline Christianity, not even a generation removed from the time of Christ, was far more complex than that of Jesus' band of twelve (or seventy-two) disciples. As thousands were added to their number daily, the necessity of establishing church offices arose (as set forth in 1 and 2 Timothy and Titus), and new theologies were needed as cultural barriers were crossed with Samaritans and Gentiles.

In the third and fourth century, via some of the early church fathers, the doctrines of the Trinity and Christ's two natures had to be articulated as some refuted them, and the Nicene Creed was adopted as a response. In the sixteenth century, the doctrine of justification by faith had to be articulated by Martin Luther as some resorted to indulgences or justification by works. In the eighteenth century, William Carey (the father of modern missions) had to write *An Enquiry*[15] to convince Protestants that the Great Commission was a missionary text, and this launched the great century of missions. In the twentieth century, the Lausanne movement penned the Lausanne Covenant, a document that became the de facto creed for what it means to be an evangelical, in which evangelism and social justice were refused into one, and the Great Reversal (when evangelicals lost the impetus for social justice) was reversed.

Until this point, the Majority World hadn't matched the theological production of the West. This was particularly due to how young some of the churches are in the Global South, so they haven't had time or resources to write theology. Partially this is due to the emphasis on orthopraxis, because writing theological tomes or creeds is not a top priority for Majority World Christians. Even among those who endeavor to do so, Majority World academic theologians are almost always concurrently serving in some sort of pastoral or missionary capacity. Bi- or trivocational pastors, missionaries, and theologians are the rule more than the exception. But just as Western evangelicalism ought to balance its orthodoxy with orthopraxis to restore purity, Majority World evangelicalism needs to increase its theological production to achieve maturity.

ECUMENICAL THEOLOGY AS A NECESSARY DEVELOPMENT

When the word *ecumenical* is mentioned, the two images most likely to be conjured up are the early church councils starting from Nicaea in AD 325 (often called, simply, the ecumenical councils) and the Edinburgh 1910 World Missionary Conference, which is often dubbed "the birthplace of the modern ecumenical movement."[16] Mark Noll lists three of these events among his top-twelve turning points in the history of the church, and they basically bookend the major turning points of the church age for him.[17]

The reason ecumenical councils or conferences are so important to the history of the church is that they are among the top producers of theology, if not *the* top. Of course, scholastic and philosophic theologians exist, and they have produced voluminous works in the recesses of dusty libraries and monasteries and ivory towers by reading about and thinking about God. But my argument is that, more than anything else, ecumenical movements have produced theology that has stood the test of time for the worldwide church. This should not be a surprise, given the fact that ecumenism implies a consensus among churches. As great as Thomas Aquinas's *Summa Theologica* or John Calvin's *Institutes* or Karl Barth's *Church Dogmatics* are, they aren't accepted widely by every faith tradition, even if Catholics rely heavily on Thomas or Reformed people love Calvin. But the Nicene Creed has near-universal acceptance.

The word *ecumenical* needs to be loosely defined here. It comes from the Greek word *oikoumene*, and for our purposes, it means "all the churches together." This doesn't necessarily mean that Catholics and Protestants and Orthodox and Pentecostals and independents must all be present for ecumenism to occur. This was certainly not the case with Edinburgh 1910, where only Protestants and a few Anglo-Catholics were present, or with Lausanne, which is wholly evangelicals, nor even with the original ecumenical councils attended only by Mediterranean Christians, who excluded Middle Eastern Christians such as Nestorians and Jacobite Monophysites as heretical.[18] I would call all of these "ecumenical" in the way I'm defining them: the unifying of a large group of Christians from different traditions and geographies or cultures, even if there isn't exhaustive representation from every part of the world.

Along with monumental ancient documents such as the Nicene Creed, modern conferences have produced important new statements of faith and purpose such as the Lausanne Covenant (for evangelicals) or the numerous documents that came out of

Vatican II (for Catholics). The important quality of ecumenical conferences, however, is that they are inherently *missional*. This means they are convened either to discuss how to reconcile disparate cultures that have joined the existing church (for example, Nicaea) or to strategize how to bring disparate cultures into the existing church (for example, Edinburgh 1910).

The very first such ecumenical council recorded in history predated Nicaea by three centuries: it was the Council of Jerusalem, mentioned in Acts 15:6-35, which took place circa AD 50. To prove my point that ecumenical councils produce substantive theology, out of the Council of Jerusalem came the first epistle found in the Bible. This was written even earlier than the Thessalonian letters, which are dated circa AD 51–52 and were written during Paul's second missionary journey. This first epistle has no name, but let's call it the letter to the Antiochenes (because James, the leader of the council, sent it to Antioch in the hands of Judas Barsabbas and Silas). We have the text of this short epistle in its entirety (its brevity even outmatches 2 and 3 John!), recounted in Acts 15:23-29:

The apostles and elders, your brothers,

To the Gentile believers in Antioch, Syria and Cilicia:

Greetings.

We have heard that some went out from us without our authorization and disturbed you, troubling your minds by what they said. So we all agreed to choose some men and send them to you with our dear friends Barnabas and Paul—men who have risked their lives for the name of our Lord Jesus Christ. Therefore we are sending Judas and Silas to confirm by word of mouth what we are writing. It

seemed good to the Holy Spirit and to us not to burden you with anything beyond the following requirements: You are to abstain from food sacrificed to idols, from blood, from the meat of strangled animals and from sexual immorality. You will do well to avoid these things.
Farewell.

Despite how short this epistle is, the theological production of the Council of Jerusalem could not have been more staggering: Gentiles are now accepted into the messianic faith without needing to subscribe to most of the Mosaic law; they need only follow the so-called Jerusalem Quadrilateral (all of which are basically pertaining to idolatry). In other words, culture (circumcision) was to be distinguished from truth (there is only one God). In the middle stands theology (human attempts to express God through language); this is the intersection where truth and culture meet. Until we get to heaven, theology—the imperfect human articulation of God—will have to do. Paul acknowledged in 1 Corinthians 13:12 that, until that time, we are merely seeing dimly in a mirror, but later we will know in full.

But this raises the chicken-and-egg problem: what comes first, theology or missions? Most evangelicals would say theology, because good evangelicals always take the Bible as our starting point. However, perhaps this is an overreaction to Catholicism, just as *sola gratia* and *sola fide* aren't completely true if taken to the furthest extreme. As the oft-quoted axiom says, "We are saved by faith alone, but the faith that saves is never alone." Works-righteousness is not the answer, but neither is cheap grace.

And the Bible was not dropped out of heaven into our laps like the Qur'an was for Muhammad or the Book of Mormon was for

Joseph Smith. Where did the Bible come from? If we are to take seriously the Chalcedonian definition of the two natures of Jesus, the living Word, as fully God and fully human, we have to also take seriously the production of the Bible, the written Word, as fully inspired by the Holy Spirit and fully written by humans.

Paul wrote half of the New Testament, for the most part *after* he completed his missionary journeys. As he encountered various cultures on his travels, that forced him to rethink his previously held Judaic worldview. The encounter with Gentiles changed him, and the Pauline epistles in turn changed the church. Only someone who had been on missions, who had to articulate the Jewish gospel continually to various Gentile cultures, could have written what he wrote.

However, there is a case to be made that theology comes before missions too. The Jerusalem Council took place *between* Paul's first and second missionary journeys. So, while Paul's first missionary journey was the impetus for the convening of the Jerusalem Council (what do they do with all the Gentiles that have now come into the faith?), the letter to the Antiochenes served as the basis for Paul's second and third missionary journeys, which in turn led to most of his other theological production (eleven of his thirteen epistles were written on his third missionary journey or during his subsequent imprisonment in Rome). So missions and theology continue this ever-cyclical dance between them, one moving forward and the other responding back, and vice versa.

This leads us to global theology, which is (based on what I just wrote) actually a tautology. Evangelicals are rightfully skittish of relativism, but at the same time we have to acknowledge that we all use our limited culture as our lenses to articulate the infinite God. There is no "absolute" theology, any more than there is an "absolute" culture. Our misguided attempts to absolutize theology have led to things such as the codification of Latin as the official holy language of the Roman Catholic Church, or—dare I say it—making the Nicene Creed the official statement of faith for all Christians for all time. To understand why universalizing the Nicene Creed is a problem, several things need to be made clear:

1. It is not that the Nicene Creed has anything in it that is wrong, per se (it is a foundational document and rightfully regarded as such!), but it is insufficient; there is a lot of important content left out. But that is the definition of a foundation: it is a good starting point, but it is not the entirety of the construction.

2. The Nicene Creed was modified from its original form at the First Ecumenical Council of Nicaea to its revised form (the Nicene-Constantinopolitan Creed) at the Second Ecumenical Council of Constantinople, so unlike Scripture, it is changeable. If it can be revised once, can it not be revised again?

3. The Nicene Creed does not have an agreed-upon form. The Roman Catholic Church insists on *filioque* (that the Holy Spirit proceeds from the Father and the Son), while the Eastern Orthodox Church does not include that word (they insist that the Holy Spirit proceeds from the Father alone). This indicates that the Nicene Creed is not infallible or universally accepted in a single iteration.

4. The Nicene Creed is very Western (by that, specifically I mean ancient Greek philosophy) in its articulation of

theology. It is also a product of a particular time in history. So it is very culturally specific by both geographical and temporal factors. Its tendency toward Platonic dualism completely leaves out Jesus' earthly life except for his birth, death, and resurrection. It is written very metaphysically, with language such as "begotten from the Father, only-begotten, that is, from the essence of the Father, God from God, light from light, true God from true God, begotten not made, of one essence with the Father."

5. A creed is not Scripture; it is a summary of what the writers deem to be the most important things found in Scripture. People today would probably emphasize different things in Scripture, depending on their culture and geography. It doesn't make them wrong; it just means that some things may not hold as much importance in one culture as they do in another. This is because the articulation of theology often arises as a response to heresy. Those who haven't encountered opposition are not forced to stake a claim for a particular point of view. This is why Andrew Walls writes in *The Missionary Movement in Christian History* that if twentieth-century Pentecostal Nigerians are shown the Nicene Creed, "they accept the creed of Nicea [*sic*], but they display little interest in it: they appear somewhat vague about the relationship of the divine Son and the Holy Spirit."[19]

Global theology is something old, but it feels like a new frontier. The first-century Christians understood that new theology must necessarily arise when encountering new cultures (Gentiles). Then we lost that understanding. Now we are regaining it. This is a good thing, as we are now starting to re-resemble the early church.

Global theology is often framed as African, Latin American, and Asian theology. This has come to the forefront of our attention because of the shift of the center of gravity of Christianity to the Majority World in the last fifty years or so. But, as we have already discussed, theology doesn't always start the conversation, so really non-Western theology has garnered widespread attention in roughly only the last ten years.

Henry Venn, the general secretary of the Church Missionary Society from 1841 to 1873, coined the name the three-self church,[20] which includes self-sustaining, self-governing, and self-propagating. Many people mistakenly think that the three-self church is only in reference to the official Chinese governmental church (called the TSPM, or the Three-Self Patriotic Movement, which started in 1951), but the phrase originated much earlier than China's appropriation of it.

However, missiologist Paul Hiebert brought up the necessity of adding a fourth self: self-theologizing.[21] Majority World churches can be "three-self" and still mimic their Western counterparts. Only when they start self-theologizing do they truly come into their own. Self-theologizing means that they start writing their own worship songs, their own creeds, and their own theology. This is meat, not milk, and it's an important later stage in the growth and maturation of Majority World churches.

We live in an exciting time. Beyond just creeds, now there is a movement toward the major production of biblical commentaries, such as the groundbreaking *Africa Bible Commentary*[22] in 2006, in which seventy African scholars (perhaps inspired by the Septuagint) commented on every book of the Bible from solely African perspectives; the *South Asia Bible Commentary*[23] of 2015; and soon the *Latin America Bible Commentary*. Majority World evangelicalism is moving in the right direction; there just needs to be more of this, which will take time.

Perhaps publishing books, journal articles, or tracts—the impetus for revolutions such as the Protestant Reformation—is not as much the way social movements arise today. Maybe social media, such as blogs and hashtag movements and YouTube videos, are a more effective way to inculcate new ideas, foment positive change, and inspire good works. However it is done, evangelicals in the Majority World need a proportional voice of influence in the world. Western evangelicals, while now the minority among the world's Christians, still wield the majority of the power in terms of ideas and resources.

CONCLUSION: THE WAY FORWARD

This chapter is called "Theology and Orthopraxis in Global Evangelicalism." I did not title it "*Orthodoxy* and Orthopraxis in Global Evangelicalism," although that would have been more parallel. The problem with the Majority World isn't a lack of true theology; it is a lack of enough theological output. It's a matter of quantity, not quality.

I also didn't title this chapter "Theology and *Action* in Global Evangelicalism," although that would have also been more parallel, because the problem with Western evangelicals is not lack of doing; it is where the energy is focused. The efforts spent on defending our turf in the culture wars could be better served in loving our neighbor as ourselves. As Biola University President Barry Corey often says, "The kind life, the receivable life, errs on the side of what we're for rather than what we're against." He continues: "We need a firm center and soft edges. We need to tone down the saber rattling, the fist shaking, the scowled conversations, the voice raising. The way of kindness is not just having right theology; it's being the right kind of people. It's understanding that our lives as Jesus' followers mean we have a common humanity with everyone, and therefore there's no need for exceptionalism. We owe all human beings the honor due them as beings made in the image of God."[24]

In order for Western and Majority-World evangelicalism to cohere, several things need to happen. First, Westerners need another reformation. As we celebrate the five-hundredth anniversary of Luther's nailing the Ninety-Five Theses to the church door at Wittenberg, we need to return to the way of Jesus. We need to stop resembling the Pharisees and focus more on the marginalized: on black and brown people who are dying, on refugees, on immigrants, on the poor. We need to act justly, love mercy, and walk humbly with our God.

Second, the Majority World needs to produce more theology. Written production stands the test of time, like the Bible; missionaries pass away, like Paul. For all of the apostles' church-planting successes in Asia Minor, Turkey today is mainly a Muslim nation. Paul's greatest lasting legacy is his thirteen epistles, which continue to convert Christians millennia after his time. But in order for the Majority World to publish, they need money, resources such as printers, and training/education such as seminaries. This is where the West can help partner to make it happen.

In addition, the West ought to celebrate this theological production and not be suspicious of it. Duane Elmer, former professor at Trinity Evangelical Divinity School, charged Christians to think beyond "right" and "wrong" and acknowledge a third category: "different."[25] Unfortunately, many Western evangelicals think that everything different is simply wrong. But multiculturalism isn't the same as heresy. Westerners need to be more open to learning from the Majority World because for far too long the teaching only went one way. Creeds and books need to be exchanged in both directions.

And finally, evangelicals worldwide need unity. We need to recognize our commonalities and not just our differences. We need to acknowledge that we all need each other and that diversity is a beautiful thing. Global evangelicalism has a strong, bright future, but only if we all work together. We have much more in common than it may seem at first glance, and that is our strength.

7

REMAINING TO REFORM

SANDRA MARIA VAN OPSTAL

In community, we braved the evening of the election of 2016. I was with a group of young Asian American professionals I had mentored. Many of them were attending a local Evangelical Covenant Church and engaging their faith on both a personal and societal level.

As the election results unfolded, we vented, we told jokes, and finally we were left in silence. Silence is not something I do well, but that evening nothing was left to be said.

Could it be that the country where our parents worked so hard to thrive had elected someone who would actively fight against our existence here? Could it be that an overwhelming majority of people who claim "one Lord, one baptism" would support a leader whose campaign was anti-immigrant, anti-refugee, and anti-Muslim? Could our brothers and sisters in the faith actually endorse an unapologetically white supremacist, nationalistic candidate accused of violating women? Yes.

Silence.

As someone who had given two decades of her life to the ministry of reconciliation, I felt *I* had failed. The evangelical space that I loved and had spent twenty years influencing, forming, and shaping was betraying my communities of color. The evangelical space that had invited my singing and passionate preaching hadn't accepted the content of my message. Speaking at college chapels, writing books on diversity and mission, training short-term missions teams, and consulting with churches had been a waste.

What was the purpose of difficult conversations with fellow believers—in which I was consistently offended—if the dial had not moved? Many of the same people that had been sending missions teams to "help the poor" of Mexico, Dominican Republic, Turkey, and Uganda were the same people who were now shouting, "Build the wall!" It was no longer just intuition; concrete data supported our experience of ethnocentric nationalism built on the wings of not only national security but also xenophobia.

The context of the 2016 election was as important as the election results themselves. The landscape for people of color was one of fear. At my church we overheard our seven- and eight-year-old congregants coach one another on the rules of answering the door to Immigration and Customs Enforcement (in our sanctuary city), and we held them as they cried in fear that their parents would be taken away.

The Syrian refugee crisis was taking place against the backdrop of anti-Islamic sentiment. The Dakota Access Pipeline was endangering the land of the Lakota people, as proven by a leak of a pipeline in South Dakota. And the militarized reaction of our government was showing how far it was willing to go to continue to take land from native peoples. The fight for immigration reform, which was hopeful in 2014, was stalled due to anti-immigrant rhetoric from Trump supporters. This was all on top of the horrendous reality of police brutality against unarmed black men and women, prompting the community to develop #BlackLivesMatter and #SayHerName movements. The experience of people of color in 2016 was an experience of faith in the midst of fear.

The "Christianized" ideology of success and security for the 81 percent of white evangelicals who voted for Trump sealed the fear and terror in the lives of my community members. These aren't issues in books or blogs. These are people who I care for deeply, people who have names: Michal, Myriam, Juwaan, Marisol, and Siouxsan. These are neighbors, congregants, community members, and friends I've met on the road to reconciliation.

My social location gives me access not only to the experiences of my people and their struggle for immigration reform and human rights, but also to those of other communities of color. Our faith should inform our location, but the reality is that our social location shapes our understanding of faith. For the 81 percent, their Western European, white, middle-class location of power has shaped them to value success and security. This is in contrast to a biblical narrative that is all about the disenfranchised and the alien. Their lack of proximity to my community, which experiences marginalization, allows them to blissfully call their idolatry "faith-filled," "pure" evangelicalism.

On November 12, 2016, the weekend after the election, *Saturday Night Live* did a sketch called "Election Night." (Stop reading and watch it if you can.) The enlightened white people are holding onto hope as they watch state by state vote for Trump. The two black performers, Chris Rock and Dave

Chappelle, continue to laugh and look at one another as the white people are shocked and dismayed. At the end of the skit, when the election is called for Trump, one of the "woke" white people says, "Oh my god, I think America is racist!"

Dave replies, "I remember my great-grandpa told me something like that."

Then a white woman says, "This is the most shameful thing America has ever done!" as Chris and Dave look at one another, laughing.

Christians of color aren't surprised that America is racist, which is why this political satire resonates with us. Christians of color couldn't have expected anything different from white evangelicals, who come from the same line of folks who were elders in white churches supporting the institutions of slavery and Jim Crow. The 2016 election clarified that we are not postracial and that the white evangelical church is more racist than its liberal counterparts. I remember my *abuelita* telling me something like that.

ON THE MARGINS OF EVANGELICALISM

When I hear the word *evangelical*, I think of someone else. As a second-generation Latina born to immigrants from Colombia and Argentina in the late seventies who was born again in a Southern Baptist church, discipled in an evangelical parachurch movement, and trained in an Evangelical Free seminary, you'd think I'd identify strongly with the use of the word. It's the spiritual heritage of my rebirth and the tradition where my immediate family members find themselves even today. It's not that I can't include myself with evangelicals. Rather, evangelicals have not sought to include me.

Isolation and *exclusion* describe my experience as a woman of color in evangelicalism. I used to believe this was because of my lack of credentials. It seemed that no matter what our expertise and experience, people like me (women of color) haven't been sought out as must-have voices in the dialogue on the future of the church, despite women being the majority of the church and, as people of color, making up the future of the church. Even after earning a master of divinity degree and decades of ministry leadership, my experience is the same.

Conferences claim to have "the best worship leaders," "the most powerful preachers," "the leaders of the future church," "the innovators in church leadership," and "the best data on millennials" that centers on the voices and therefore perspectives of white upper-middle-class men in suits or skinny pants. The way they interpret data, the ideas that evolve, and their forms of leadership are socially located and not at all effective in my context.

To take our multiethnic leaders to a conference to learn from people who have no idea what it means to pastor in a community of trauma or fear would be frustrating, to say the least. Not far from this, the "diversity formula" is at work in many progressive conferences. It's tokenizing at best when, among ten speakers, there is only one white woman (the storyteller), one black man (the entertainer), one black woman (diversity talk), one Asian man (professor type), and six white men. It's the equivalent of the caricatures in the ABC television show *Modern Family*. The white evangelical industrial complex is full of exclusion.

White evangelical institutions "allow" people of color to lead in reconciliation, justice, missions, urban ministry, and minority departments. These same institutions "allow" women to lead and write only for women, even when we have broad expertise in worship, theology, evangelism, formation, and leadership. When a woman writes an article about contextualized preaching or worship, her book is branded "women's." When a male writes it, his book is labeled "preaching" or "leadership."

Even when we are "allowed" to lead, it must be done in ways that reflect white cultural values, expressions, and sensibilities. Sadly, many of us internalize our oppression because we are happy to be asked to participate. Our experience of extended periods of exclusion, even after all of the credentialing, makes us feel like we should be honored to have been invited to lead. But, in fact, it should be a relationship of mutuality.

Going to seminary was a daily frustration. I was the only woman in many of my classes, and I could count the number of Latinx students on one hand, most being Latin American international scholars. They were great friends, but they didn't share my experience. (Latinx is the gender-neutral alternative to Latino and Latina used by scholars, activists, and journalists.) Despite the tens of thousands of pages I read while in seminary, I was never assigned a book by an ethnic minority scholar, let alone a Latinx theologian.

My community's spirituality and perspectives were excluded as I learned about the history of Christianity. We skipped right from the early church to linger for months in the European white saviors of the Reformation and then moved on to the white saviors of the great revivals. I was a younger leader in the Lausanne Evangelical movement, so I knew that mission was "from everywhere to everywhere." According to my professors' lectures, we Latinx are always the mission field in need of more salvation. I never learned that we are actually a mission force, particularly in countries that are closed to white evangelicals.

In preparation for the pastorate, I was never influenced by someone who came from my location. I never heard our voice in the classroom, and even worse, my classmates never heard the voice of my community. Yes, I was on the margins.

My blood type is O negative, so I am the universal donor—a blood bank's dream. A universal donor can give to anyone, so hospital shelves are lined with O negative. The reverse is not true; the universal donor can receive only O negative blood. In seminary, I learned that the universal theological donor is a white evangelical. This donor is always translating books into other languages, planting churches in other countries, setting up seminaries on other continents, and sending professors to teach global Christians. And this donor never seems to receive from the global church.

White evangelicals wouldn't say directly that they have nothing to learn from Latinx, African American, Asian American, or Native scholars—but they don't notice when our voices are absent. Some wouldn't publicly deny that women have much to offer to the practices of the church, but they assign books by men in their leadership classes and don't see how detrimental that is to the formation of future pastors. Even the most supportive and well-meaning teachers I've had excluded voices of women and communities of color from my education.

I recently discovered my own complicity when I was forced to condense my library. As my ministry partner, an Iranian-Korean woman helped me to purge my shelves. We created stacks and stacks of books that were all from the universal theological donor. If a woman of color who is intentional about the books she buys and the voices she seeks to be influenced by doesn't notice the one-sided influence, imagine how much less this is noticed by the broader evangelical world.

I was told that attending a white evangelical seminary would be challenging, but the relationships built there were needed to humanize the people behind those perspectives. It taught me that, even among leaders in a conservative, white evangelical theological movement that oppresses women and tokenizes people of color, there are God-fearing men who have been shaped by their circumstances, not just their will. My wise mentor knew this and suggested I receive theological training in that context. It served to remind me that white men aren't my enemies but family, even if I'd rather not claim them. This in no way excuses the patriarchy and colonization I and other women of color have had to endure, but it helps me to know how the social location of white men has shaped them.

One memorable experience of this was when my ethics professor assigned immigration as one of our mandatory topics. He later recanted because a student had expressed a desire to study something more "relevant." The professor released the class from having to consider the ethics behind welcoming the stranger in pursuit of something else. The one time we were finally going to engage in something that was meaningful to my Latinx community, it was marginalized to the place of "optional." My classmates' and professor's location and context hadn't put them in proximity to people affected directly by our antiquated immigration policies. They didn't pastor my neighbors, so how could they know that all of the trendy work they were doing with sex trafficking was directly related to the vulnerability of undocumented women?

Recently I had the honor of hearing stories of undocumented women in sanctuary in New York City. As they shared, we realized that I had not set any ground rules on the use of media.

A person in the audience asked me if he could use the names and pictures of the women on social media, noting that his organization had ten million followers. I replied, "No, we don't want to endanger them."

But one of the women, Judith, exclaimed, "I am here, I am human, I have a name, I have a story: Tell it!" Undocumented immigrants, and especially dreamers, find their power in moving from the shadows to the light. Our lament as evangelicals of color is that we are unseen and undervalued. We are not voiceless—just unheard.

A CALLING TO WAKE THE SLEEPING

I was in a bookstore, exhausted from preaching, when I felt someone gazing at me. I turned to look and was almost pounced on by a middle-aged blonde woman. With dried tears evident on her face, she exclaimed, "Thank you for teaching me. Thank you for telling me. Thank you for waking me up. I've been going to church for decades, and I never knew." She paused and looked at me for a minute and added, "I think I was sleeping."

Despite the experience of being excluded, forgotten, or marginalized, I am evangelical because this was the expression of faith that nurtured and raised me. I wasn't born into it, and I'm not quite sure I've been fully accepted or adopted, but I am in the system.

I can't speak for every woman of color or for every Latinx believer about whether they should align themselves with a system that consistently marginalizes them. But I know the Lord has orchestrated this for me. I know this level of loyalty and communalism is rooted in both my ethnic cultural values and my ecclesiology. And my ecclesiology has been shaped by my Latinx cultural values. Latinx families stay and fight—and healthy ones fight well. Commitment can't be abandoned because of differences.

Evangelicalism is also the place I'm most effective. My familiarity with evangelical values, culture, and institutions allows me to serve in re-centering or reorienting us.

On that day that I met the blonde woman, I had stood on the plenary stage of the Justice Conference in front of a primarily white audience and told them that they needed my community. I tried with as much integrity as I could to tell the stories of the mothers and fathers in my community whose families were being ripped apart by our unchristian, inhumane immigration system. I shared about the spirituality of the Latinx community and the courage and faith they could bring to bear on the anemic faith of their white brothers and sisters.

Part of white evangelical culture is that the message should always be positive, encouraging, and safe for the whole family. I believed my message had been so offensive there was no way they would invite me back. When I finished speaking, I turned to my husband and said, "I think I just got in trouble." But the opposite was true. Dozens of people thanked me for challenging them to live into their faith differently and to take more seriously the call of Christ toward compassion and justice. Person after person shared how deeply transformed they were by the new revelation that fighting for justice was not only for the liberation of the oppressed people but for their own liberation as well.

Later that day, I received calls from church leaders as well as from one woman whose story I shared. They expressed how proud they were of me and how honored they were that I had given voice to our community. Pastor John Zayas, the senior pastor of my church, Grace and Peace Community, encouraged me to continue with courage in making our stories known. He said, "That is your calling, Sandra. You are our voice. You are part of us, you live here, love here, and you take our passion and insight and make it known to people who would never listen to us."

I'm staying in my evangelical family with the hope that we can be reformed. My desire is that the communities that have historically been overlooked, marginalized, or intentionally ignored will be restored and given a place of honor. I am here to remind my family that the global church has moved from the west to the south.

REMAINING TO REFORM

Why stay? I ask myself that same question daily. At least weekly since the election, I've ask my husband why I should stay within evangelical institutions and circles. As if the posts on social media by white evangelicals weren't enough to make me want to leave, belonging to a community of people that doesn't acknowledge my community's existence sure does. So again, why claim a community that doesn't claim me or mine?

I stay because I am evangelical in my beliefs. I hold to the authority of Scripture and the importance of teaching Scripture as a way of formation. I was taught to exposit Scripture before I ever called myself a preacher. Grace and Peace Community is a part of the Christian Reformed Church of North America, although we are culturally reforma-costal. We preach the Word to instruct and inspire. We believe the Word is living and active and can penetrate our hearts and minds and cause us to change. We believe it is historical, true, and authoritative. *#evangelical*

I believe every human created in God's image is given an opportunity to turn to him in repentance for salvation. I believe that by God's grace we are saved and delivered. I believe that apart from a relationship with God we are spiritually dead, no matter how many good deeds we perform. At Grace and Peace Community we have altar calls at least twice a month. We can't keep up with the amount of people that come to faith. *#evangelical*

Actively living out faith in Jesus is central to my calling as a mission and justice mobilizer. Because of my belief that faith expresses itself in action and calls others to Jesus and his kingdom, I've led teams of people to Egypt, Dominican Republic, South Africa, China, and Capitol Hill. That is why Grace and Peace Community has a food co-op, a shelter, an after-school program, hurricane relief efforts, and evangelistic outreach to the community. *#evangelical*

The uniqueness and centrality of the life, death, resurrection, and return of Jesus is what we celebrate as a community when we come to the table. I pastor at the intersection of creeds and the movement of the Holy Spirit. I serve in a community of pastors of color who believe the good news of Jesus can reorient, revive, and renew us. *#evangelical*

I'm able to remain in the broader evangelical community because I don't worship in a white church. I worship in a multi-ethnic, multiclass, and multigenerational community. Only about 10 percent of my church is white, which means they submit to the authority of leaders of color. This is extremely rare. My weekly worship isn't disrupted by the idolatry I'm exposed to in the work I do as a speaker, consultant, and mobilizer of reconciliation.

At Grace and Peace Community, vulnerable people help vulnerable people. The undocumented woman cares for the survivor of domestic violence. The formerly incarcerated lead disaster relief to the islands for which we conveniently forgot we were responsible. I'm surrounded by people who are serious about Jesus, passionate about God's kingdom, and filled with the Holy Ghost. They send me, they cover me in prayer, and they patch me back together when I return from war with the evil that seeks to devour the church.

I'm often ashamed and angered by my evangelical family in the United States, but it doesn't cause me to leave—it causes me to speak up and speak out. Evangelicalism is about conversion, reform, transformation, and repentance. If I'm going to remain, I'm going to use my voice for reform. I'm going to take seriously how the authoritative Word of God speaks to the racism and xenophobia of our evangelical family. As I stay faithful to a local congregation and in submission to a community, I continue to hope transformation can happen. I'm remaining to reform because I believe not only in the gospel of Christ but also in the work of the Holy Spirit to free us from bondage and revive us.

I remain because as much as I want freedom for my own— those in my socioeconomic and cultural community—I want freedom for white, well-meaning Christians too. And it's not as if the church wasn't already broken! From the time of Scripture until today, idolatry, greed, and pride have been rampant in the church. The journey of God's people has always been one step forward, three steps back—with a lot of prophets in between who were silenced and killed. Even if there is just a tiny remnant in the 81 percent, I will remain to reform.

I remain at great cost, along with other people of color. We pay on both sides. On the one hand, we pay the cost of enduring the white supremacy and patriarchy of white evangelical culture. We endure constant marginalization and mansplaining (when a man restates what a woman says to help others understand her, depreciating her contribution). We endure being seen as people of color or as angry women who need to learn to forgive and love more. On the other hand, we pay the cost of being seen as sellouts in our own community. From those who have lost respect for our choice to reclaim or reform evangelicalism, we endure calls to *#getfree*. We pay the cost for the remnant.

On a recent advocacy visit to Capitol Hill with a group of evangelical women, at three appointments in a row, the representative or aid with whom we met expressed surprise that we were evangelical. They didn't know that evangelicals cared about immigration and human rights, and they didn't think such a diverse group of women could be evangelical. The level of surprise was more than what I had witnessed on my previous visit in 2015, and that solidified my call to remain evangelical. If the people who hold the power in our government think that evangelicals are a homogeneous group made up of white, male, Republican, anti-immigrant, anti-women, anti-gay, pro-self-interest people, then the witness of the church is at stake.

INAUGURATION DAY

When Latinx hear the word *evangelical*, they think of someone else. I don't know any people in my community, brown or black, on the west side of Chicago that would call themselves evangelical. Some might say, "We're not evangelical, *somos evangelicos*." This isn't merely a translation of the word into Spanish; it is a different expression of faith.

White missionaries from evangelical persuasions brought the message of the gospel to Latin America, and my people made it their own. Free of white control, Latinx church leaders in cities and villages, both educated and not, made it their own by the power of the Holy Spirit. Without white theological institutions to colonize their faith expressions, the authority of Scripture coupled with a power encounter with the Spirit gave freedom for a contextualized theology to emerge. *Evangelicos* are planting vibrant churches that are thriving in difficult social locations. Latinx, like other people of color, are experiencing revival and growth while many white evangelicals are not. Every time I hear about how churches are shrinking and the number of young people in evangelicalism is declining, I'm bothered because that's not the full story.

It is said that, in the first three centuries, love so characterized the entire church that Roman society took note. Tertullian reported that the Romans would exclaim, "See how they love one another."[1] Justin Martyr recounted that they moved from wealth, success, and security to caring for those in need. A devastating plague swept across the ancient world in the third century, and Christians were the only ones who cared for the sick, even at the risk of contracting the plague themselves. People were throwing infected members of their own families into the streets, even before they died, in order to protect themselves from the disease. There were no medical mission organization or denominational church-growth programs; there was just the church. Maybe this is why Christianity spread rapidly. The love practiced by Christians drew the attention of the world, just as Jesus said it would. *Somos evangelicos.*

The accounts of the early church sound a lot like our community churches to me—churches such as Grace and Peace Community, where 150 adults and fifty children are able to send cargo planes and semis full of supplies to hurricane victims in

Texas, Mexico, and Puerto Rico. I think about the neighborhood reach of Canaan Community Church in Englewood, Illinois, and the work they're doing to change the way people view African American communities. I think about New Life La Villita's sports camps and work with Chicago-area youth on parole to keep them from entering prison.

These are all evangelicals of color serving with their communities—loving, learning, and working to show unconditional compassion and love. We don't have time for arguments about atonement theory—we are trying to save lives. As I was finalizing this chapter, one of my friends was denied asylum and is likely to be sent back to the most dangerous country in Central America. One friend was beaten and threatened by her boyfriend. And one youth was incarcerated for murder. That is my pastoral reality, the context in which some of our evangelical communities are thriving.

Unless white evangelical churches plan to reach only certain ZIP codes, they will need the help of their brothers and sisters of color who have expertise in reaching out to, ministering to, and walking with ethnic minority communities. If every conference on church planting, evangelism, worship, and preaching features only white male speakers as teachers, white evangelicals will not be prepared to do church. They will only continue to excel at developing services and communities that are conducive to white, upper-middle-class, educated, and primarily suburban folks.

While I know there are movements (conferences, academia, publishing) that have a desire to include women and ethnic minorities, I haven't seen many who put Latinx on the mainstage. We tend to be relegated to speaking on niche topics like reconciliation, outreach to Latinx communities, and immigration; we aren't given space to shape the framework of the conversation on universal themes such as evangelism. Without the entire body, the church can't move forward with more creative perspectives on mission and discipleship.

Ethnic minority churches are thriving in the midst of scarcity, developing young leaders well, and leading the way in "telling the story" (as we come from oral cultures). But no one sits at our feet. The white evangelical church will miss out on a lot if we don't grow beyond token representation. *#tokenism* This is why I'm committed to both naming the problem and submitting myself to displacement experiences that most of my peers would decline. There is hope for evangelicalism, and that hope is us.

In community, we braved Inauguration Day of 2017. I happened to be on the East Coast with a group of women of color who have dedicated their lives to reconciliation and justice. These women, who are national voices, authors, professors, pastors, and movement leaders, sat together in solidarity and witnessed evangelicals in our country celebrate the leadership of a man who has emboldened white supremacists that had been lurking in private places. Since the election, it had become clear that some people who claim faith in Jesus feel confident and justified in spewing violence toward our communities.

We felt so violated by our "family" that we couldn't bring ourselves to speak. Silence. Again.

The purpose of our meeting was to plan a gathering to empower women of color. Instead we left with no plans to ever gather again. One by one, the women expressed that white evangelicalism is dead and that they would be moving on to follow Jesus apart from the 81 percent. I understood, but I wasn't ready to leave.

I took a walk with a friend after our formal meetings ended and expressed that I also wondered how God could be in anything so vile and violent against people of color made in God's image. I too was grieved and angered that the 81 percent would give power to a man who planned to annihilate my people with one policy or another. I too wanted to leave. I've thought about that walk many times since that day.

I have also prayed this prayer many times: "Lord, is white evangelicalism dead?"

I have very little interest in spending time and energy to resuscitate the corpses within white evangelicalism. However, I do believe there is a remnant of people worth engaging. Whatever needs to die, let it die. We need death and resurrection. We need revival.

8

LOOKING FOR UNITY IN ALL THE WRONG PLACES

MARK GALLI

When I think about the evangelical family, I think about Dmitri, Ivan, and Alyosha, the three siblings in *The Brothers Karamazov*. They are as different as different can be, and yet, to author Fyodor Dostoyevsky, they each represent a crucial trait of the Russian people.

Dimitri, the eldest, fluctuates between two extremes. He longs for honor and nobility while struggling to tame dishonorable and ignoble impulses. For example, he lusts after Katherine and lays plans to get her alone in his room. But when she arrives, his better self takes over and he refuses to seduce her.

Ivan is the family intellectual. His studies have made him deeply concerned about human suffering. He can't reconcile God's goodness and power with the presence of so much injustice in the world. So he remains both bitter and morose throughout the novel.

The youngest son, Alyosha, is deeply religious and attractive, and everyone seems to love him. He moves among all manner of people and performs quiet acts of kindness and love. He is not a perfect Christ figure, but his failures only illuminate his loving personality.

Dostoyevsky makes no attempt to harmonize these three but simply describes them in their stark differences. The conflicted Dimitri, the bitter Ivan, the loving Alyosha—these are all sons of one father, and also sons of Mother Russia.

If there is no Russianism—only Russian people, Russian governments, Russian literature, and so forth—there is no evangelicalism. Scholars who study evangelicals are usually quick to acknowledge this. There is no evangelical Vatican, no organization that speaks for all evangelicals, no evangelical creed to which we all subscribe, no annual festival we attend, no evangelical holy days. As soon as we start talking about evangelicalism, we're talking about something in the abstract, and evangelicals are anything but abstract.

On the other hand, there are indeed evangelical colleges with evangelical professors and students. There are evangelical humanitarian organizations and evangelical mission societies and evangelical publishing houses and evangelical pastors and churches—and so on. Putting it this way helps us see through the fog of abstraction to how evangelical Christians actually live, breathe, and work.

As soon as we make the switch from *evangelicalism* the noun to *evangelical* the adjective, we immediately recognize that there are many evangelicalisms. The variety of evangelical Christians is not unlike the variety of brothers or characters in the great Russian novel, and the variety among evangelicals rivals that of the many cultures created by God at the tower of Babel.

That biblical story, in fact, is not a bad way to understand evangelical variety and all its confusions. So varied are we, we can hardly understand one another at times. It's as if we're each speaking a different language. That was certainly the shock some evangelicals felt after the election of Donald Trump, especially when they heard that 81 percent of white evangelicals voted for him. Most evangelical Christians like me exclaimed, "Who are these people? I know hardly anyone, let alone any evangelical Christian, who voted for Trump."

■ ■ ■

I describe evangelicals like me as "elite" evangelicals. As Joan Williams put it in *Working Class: Overcoming Class Cluelessness in America*, "It's not a term many Americans are comfortable with." But, she says, if "you are part of the professional-managerial class, well, you're an elite."[1] While she goes on to add income levels to her definition, such a class distinction doesn't require it for my purposes here. To call such evangelicals elite doesn't mean we are superior in any way, only that we are a distinct social class, mostly defined by being leaders in evangelical institutions and movements. We have better access to the levers of mass communication than do most evangelicals. We're the kind of people who join in writing books about evangelicals, and we speak at conferences marketed to evangelicals. Some assume that "elite" equals white, but no longer. Go to most evangelical gatherings, and you'll find a fair number of African American, Asian, and Hispanic speakers leading workshops and plenary sessions. Nonwhite authors are now common in evangelical publishing efforts.

And this class of evangelicals has discovered that we have family members so different they seem like aliens in our midst. These other evangelicals often haven't finished college, and if they have jobs (and apparently a lot of them don't), they are blue-collar jobs or entry-level work. They don't write books or give speeches; they don't attend conferences of evangelicals for social justice or evangelicals for immigration reform. They are deeply suspicious of mainstream media. And a lot of them voted for Donald Trump. (To be fair, some elite evangelicals also voted for Trump, often holding their noses when they did so. But space constraints require me to speak in broad generalities here.)

In response to their vote, some of the elite have said we feel "betrayed" by these voters. Others were so shocked and appalled they wanted to disown them and said they weren't going to describe themselves as evangelicals any longer. Some said pro-Trump evangelicals sullied the witness of the church and the name of Jesus Christ.

Even after all that has been written and said to help us better understand and even empathize with (if not agree with) Trump supporters—again, many of whom are evangelicals—we still have a very difficult time imagining they belong in the family we inhabit. One example will have to suffice.

I was asked to lead a panel at the Evangelical Press Association recently on "How the church should respond to the Trump administration." Given the composition of the panel and that of the EPA, it seemed best to focus on white evangelicals, as the division between black and white evangelicals is riddled with some unique dynamics. But even at that, when we finally invited and presented as a panel, not a single member could be said to be a Trump supporter—and this in a press association of a movement that went 81 percent for Trump. We who had organized the panel had just assumed that decent, thoughtful evangelicals wouldn't do that sort of thing.

An email from a man, Ben Schmittdiel, who listened to that EPA panel when it was the substance of a later podcast summarized well how some from this much larger and more representative group felt about the panel:

First of all I do not understand why it is OK to refer to our sitting president continually in such disdainful tones, as if spitting the name "Trump" out as an epithet. I know it is subjective, but I doubt if anyone could possibly miss the attitude that assumed that here is someone to be despised. While your panel is advocating for unknown immigrants, they express no respect or compassion for the person they do know. And this is a person who half the nation chose as their president. Is that a "Christian attitude"? Is it that hard to be respectful?

Second of all, I am quite sure for most evangelicals who voted for him, Donald Trump was not their first choice. However, thank God, he was a tremendously better choice than the alternative that *insured* expansion of abortion, a liberal agenda that would emphasize enforcement of a sexual agenda antithetical to biblical values, and continued tightening of restrictions against free practice of religion.

It seems your whole panel has put their heads in the sand to ignore what a Hillary Clinton presidency would have meant. Even the appointment of Justice Gorsuch was criticized since "we don't know yet what he will do." Does anyone doubt what a Hillary Clinton appointed justice would have done? Is there really any doubt what direction that would have taken our country and how it would have affected children both born and unborn? Yet, Donald

Trump has not only faithfully appointed a conservative justice, but has taken other measures such as renewing the Mexico City rule and doing all he can to defund Planned Parenthood. He has proven himself a serious pro-life President, and yet your panel could not bring themselves to recognize the integrity demonstrated in this area that is more important to many evangelicals than any other. . . .

All in all, the panel of self-described "thought leaders" sounded like spoiled and arrogant snobs. Everyone who does not agree with them (apparently 81 percent of evangelicals) is unbiblical, undisciplined, or unchurched and generally need to be led by those who know so much more—them. It has not occurred to them that maybe *they* are the ones out of step.

I should note how he began his email, because it summarizes well the feelings of many nonelite evangelicals: "I cannot express enough how arrogant, condescending, and even downright disrespectful I found so much of the dialog. As your panel expressed several times, how embarrassing some evangelicals attitudes were, I was embarrassed that I am identified with the people on this podcast."

This email represents many that *Christianity Today* has received over the last few months. What all this signals is this: evangelicals on the left and right are utterly embarrassed about one another, and each wants to disassociate itself from the other because of attitudes about the sitting president.

But Donald Trump as such is not the issue. His candidacy and now presidency have only revealed a rift in the evangelical world that is threatening to become an unbridgeable divide.

This isn't a happy state of affairs, but it's this very confusion and division that suggests to some that the label *evangelical* should be abandoned. I've been part of the evangelical world since the 1970s, and this turn in the conversation occurs every few years, usually driven by one scandal or extremist or another (Jimmy Swaggart, Jim Bakker, Jerry Falwell, Pat Robertson, and so on). While a name change might be a good public-relations move, it wouldn't change anything on the ground. It wouldn't help us grapple with our differing political and moral judgments, except to justify us not talking to one another. Nor would it change what makes this disparate group of evangelicals live and breathe and have their being.

Evangelicals have a long pedigree. What Puritan historian Perry Miller said about the Puritans applies in large part to evangelicals as well:

> As long as it [American Puritanism] remained alive, its real being was not in doctrines but behind them; the impetus came from an urgent sense of man's predicament, from a mood so deep that it could never be completely articulated. Inside the shell of its theology and beneath the surface coloring of it political theory, Puritanism was yet another manifestation of a piety to which some men are probably always inclined and which in certain conjunctions appeals irresistibly to large numbers of exceptionally vigorous spirits. I venture to call this piety Augustinian . . . because Augustine is the arch-exemplar of a religious frame of mind of which Puritanism is only one instance out of many in fifteen hundred years of religious history.[2]

Most evangelicals do not have the intellectual interests that characterized Puritan preachers, but they are driven by many of the same internal conflicts and passions:

> Puritan theology was an effort to externalize and systematize this subjective mood. Piety was the inspiration for Puritan heroism and the impetus in the charge of Puritan Ironsides; it also made sharp the edge of Puritan cruelty and justified the Puritan in his persecution of disagreement. It inspired Puritan idealism and encouraged Puritan snobbery. It was something that men either had or had not, it could not be taught or acquired. It was foolishness and fanaticism to their opponents, but to themselves it was life eternal. . . . It blazed most clearly and most fiercely in the person of Jonathan Edwards. . . . It cannot be presented by description; to be presented adequately there is need for a Puritan who is also a dramatic artist, and Bunyan alone fulfills the two requirements.[3]

Perry's reference to Bunyan is apropos. A few decades ago, *Christianity Today* asked leading evangelicals of the previous generation what books have most shaped them, and the one book that came up in almost every one of the lists was *The Pilgrim's Progress.*

Perhaps Puritanism is a bad example, because as a name it hardly has a positive reputation. But the point is that you can change the name, but God in his providence will continue to raise up a people of this Augustinian piety, who not only long for deliverance from sin and death, but who, transformed by the redeeming grace of Christ's work on the cross, have a passion to reform themselves, their churches, their world—and even fellow

evangelicals! Evangelicals are a restless lot, and their piety over-
flows in ways sometimes admirable and sometimes fanatical.
But it is a subjective mood and piety that isn't going anywhere
anytime soon.

■ ■ ■

It is a mood and a piety—especially the urge to reform—that
has gotten us to the confusing place we find ourselves. Having
personally lived through the era in which evangelicals become
politicized, I believe that the rise of the evangelical left in the
1970s and the evangelical right in the 1980s have played a large
part in how we apparently now redefine ourselves. The motives
of each party shouldn't be questioned, as each side felt a moral
duty to apply its faith to the public square, to reform it in what
it believed was a more biblical image.

And that was the problem: many of those on the left and the
right have begun to identify their politics as *Christian* or *biblical*
or *evangelical*. And naturally, they each were appalled when
fellow believers made different prudential judgments about
what constituted the public good. Sinners that we all are, we
assume that our party is on God's side, and the other has been
co-opted by the other political party. And thus the barbs that
say progressive evangelicals are the Democratic Party at prayer,
and the religious right, the Republican Party at prayer.

Like most Christians in most eras, we have a hard time believing we are justified by faith. So extraordinary and unbe-
lievable is the gospel, we go to extraordinary means to justify our
lives in all sorts of ways, one of which is by our politics. Thus we
have a need to identify our politics with God and virtue, and to
critique the politics of other evangelicals as grounded in fear or

ignorance. We struggle to imagine that evangelicals who lobby for the other side might in fact have cogent reasons for advocating as they do.

As a member of the evangelical elite, I happen to believe our nation should be more generous about opening its borders to refugees and immigrants. I believe that my convictions on these matters are shaped by my faith, and I'm tempted to believe that every compassionate, mature Christian would take my views.

That's why people like me are likely to assume that contrary views are not driven by prudential judgment or political reasoning but by mere prejudice and fear. It's why we put pro-immigration signs in our yard that announce, "We are not afraid," as if anyone who disagrees with us on immigration policy has a psychological problem. We also like to talk about "the culture of fear" in America, and by that we often mean people who don't agree with our politics on this and other matters.

We do this without recognizing how much fear we inadvertently display when we talk about what will happen if "those people" get in charge of the country. When pressed about this, we argue that our fears are rational, and the fears of the other side are not.

The rhetorical use of fear to score political points highlights how little empathy we have for people of different views. If our loved ones express fear, we are quick to sympathize with them, to comfort them, to gently prod them out of their fear. But when we suspect fellow evangelicals are fearful, we use their fear as a weapon. We announce that at least "we are not afraid," suggesting that fear is a moral failing—and certainly not one we share.

To be fair, conservatives, for their part, play the same game, using an emotional state as a weapon. They often accuse liberals

of being "bleeding hearts," having no hardheaded compre-
hension about how the real world works. In other words, liberals
don't have cogent reasons for their views; they are just flighty
people driven by emotion.

Once we've committed to one political position or another, we
have a difficult time not believing that our politics are God's
politics. It becomes harder and harder to acknowledge that politics is a messy business, that one has to make all sorts of moral
and strategic compromises to make any headway, that there are
no Christian politics but only Christians who act politically, based
on convictions surely shaped by their faith, but nearly all the time
driven by prudential judgments about the best way forward, judgments based often on the fickle nature of people and events.

When we find ourselves in such a place, we would do well to
remember our first love, Jesus Christ, and his saving work on the
cross and his redeeming love for the world. By God's grace, this
is, in fact, what most evangelicals do.

■ ■ ■

Yet this is precisely the problem of the secular media; they have
lost sight of the first love of the vast majority of evangelicals. For
much of the media, politics is about religion; they think their job
is to determine who is on what side by the votes people cast. Thus
we see a constant stream of surveys that tell us what evangelicals
believe about this burning political issue or that, which candidate
they support, and so on. It slowly but surely leaves the impression
that evangelicals—when they go about their day, when they come
to church, when they attend small groups, when they sit on church
committees—see themselves first and foremost as political crea-
tures whose lives are shaped and directed by the politics they hold.

There is no question that some evangelical churches have been politicized, both on the left and on the right. But, in fact, most evangelicals are driven by something other than politics; they find their identity not in a party but in a person, and the person is not a candidate or the president. Yes, of course, some do; that's because they are sinners and are subject to one idolatry or another. Which of us isn't? But mostly evangelicals think of themselves as Jesus people, those who trust in Jesus Christ as their Lord and Savior and who seek to live their lives day to day for him.

Most days, those lives are consumed with being faithful spouses and parents, being diligent and honest in their jobs, caring for their children, teaching Sunday school, volunteering at the food pantry, attending a small-group Bible study, and reading their Bible and praying for guidance and strength, trying to find opportunities to share their faith with others. They also happen to be Americans, so they know they have a responsibility to vote; so, yes, they have political opinions. But these are only one part of a much larger picture of who they are and how they understand themselves.

One reason most evangelicals object to politics entering the church—either through the pulpit or through advocacy groups in the church—is that they understand how quickly politics can derail the devotion of the church to Jesus Christ. They say, "Politics are divisive," and we assume they mean they just don't like conflict. But evangelicals love conflict, as the number of church splits testifies! And while they will start and sustain a fight over theology or ethics (and the accompanying personality conflicts that are part of that), they hesitate to start a church fight over civics, because they recognize how easily it can distract us from our first love.

This doesn't mean that every evangelical Christian holds mature moral and political views. When it comes to any church, we are wise to recall what Jesus told us long ago: the church is full of wheat and tares. It contains immature and mature believers. It has in its midst some foolish people and some wise people. It has sinners and saints. And it can count each of these in the elite and in the nonelite classes of evangelicals. Spiritual maturity is no respecter of class.

And so we come to ecclesiology: what we believe about the church and our obligations to the church—in this case, to the evangelical church.

I have noted how evangelicals left and right find themselves embarrassed by those on the other side of the political aisle. Such evangelicals also say that the other evangelicals sully the name *evangelical* and even the reputation of Jesus Christ. This usually means that these differing evangelicals have different unbelieving Americans they're trying to impress with the gospel, and when it becomes known that some evangelicals take a different political tack, well, it's embarrassing to the cause. How will they know that Jesus is someone they should be open to if people like *that*, who identify with Jesus' name, vote like *that*?

Then again, when Jesus prayed for his disciples, he said this:

> I pray also for those who will believe in me through their message, that all of them may be one, Father, just as you are in me and I am in you. May they also be in us so that the world may believe that you have sent me. I have given them the glory that you gave me, that they may be one as we are one—I in them and you in me—so that they may be brought to complete unity. Then the world will know

that you sent me and have loved them even as you have loved me. (John 17:20-23)

According to our Lord, it isn't our politics that will convince the world of the truth of Jesus Christ, but when we transcend our politics, when we demonstrate our unity with him and with one another—in short, when we love one another even as Jesus loved us.

It was while we were sinners—weak, stupid, immoral, politically corrupt, prideful, arrogant, elitist, racist, misogynist, thieving, murderous, and so on and so forth—that he lived among us and died for us. He didn't consider it above himself to be identified with this motley crew of humanity. In fact, in his day, these were those whom respectable people despised, who sullied his reputation when he spent time in their homes. But Jesus was willing to risk his reputation to love people no matter where they were morally, ethically, or politically.

He not only lived with and among such people, he was willing to go the distance for them, enduring the humiliation of arrest and trial, and the unimaginable pain of crucifixion.

After his death and resurrection, he sent his Holy Spirit to establish his church. Instead of a gathering of perfect saints, mature in morals and wise in politics, he gathered into his church prideful, competitive, divisive individuals who had to be told constantly to love one another. Among them were gossips and the lazy and even those who practiced the most scandalous of sexual immoralities. And on this rather unseemly body of people he puts his mark, his brand. He wants the world to know them as "the church of Jesus Christ," to know that this disreputable group is his representative in the world.

This is the church of Jesus Christ today, and it includes evangelicals. Our portion of the universal church, like all others, is full of sinners and saints—spiritually, morally, and politically. Certainly there are justifiable reasons to leave the evangelical family, especially if Augustinian piety is no longer a driving force in one's life or if one begins to identify more fully with another Christian tradition. But leaving because we simply find one another politically obtuse—well, let's not forget that Jesus called both a revolutionary zealot and a Roman collaborator to be part of the Twelve. (I would have loved to hear Simon the zealot and Matthew the tax collector go at it late into the night.)

To be sure, the fact that we're a mixture of foolish and wise, immature and mature doesn't end the matter. Every generation has the ongoing challenge of discipleship, so that more and more disciples might grow into the full stature of Christ (which includes learning wise and humble engagement in the public square). The grace of Christ not only gathers this motley group called the church but also makes possible our transformation.

But let's not kid ourselves that this sort of thing happens in a lifetime or that the church, this side of the kingdom, will be rid of arrogance or ignorance—and thus the need for forbearance and charity toward one another.

In the meantime, we would do well to ask for the Holy Spirit to come upon us so that even if we still fail to understand the language of the other, we can hear them speak about the wonders of God in their own tongues (Acts 2:11). And one of the greatest wonders is the gospel of grace and reconciliation in Jesus Christ, who bridges the most unimaginable divides and makes the disparate and mutually suspicious nothing less than sisters and brothers.

EVANGELICALISM MUST BE BORN AGAIN

SHANE CLAIBORNE

For much of my life, I've been pretty comfortable being associated with the word *evangelical*. After all, the original Greek word *euangelion* from which we derive the word *evangelical* means "good news," and I love spreading the good news of Jesus.

I embrace the core beliefs that have defined evangelicalism historically—things like a personal relationship with Jesus, salvation by the grace of God, a love for the Bible as God's Word, a commitment to the local church, and so on.

And yet, while I believe many of the things, I find myself at odds with the things that have come to characterize contemporary evangelicalism in America. To be frank, my commitment to Jesus has put me at odds with evangelicalism. While I may love what evangelicalism has been in the past, I am grieved by what it has become.

Christians in America in general have an image problem. When the Barna Group polled the country and asked young non-Christians what their perceptions of Christians were, the top responses were (1) antigay, (2) judgmental, and (3) hypocritical. The rest of the list didn't get much better. People said Christians are "too political" and that we are irrelevant.

What broke my heart even more than what people said was what people did not say. The very thing that Jesus said the world would know we are Christians by—love—didn't even register on the chart. Nor did the fruit of the Spirit—those beautiful things that God is like: joy, peace, patience, kindness, goodness, faithfulness, self-control, and love. It's clear that we have become known for some of the very things that Jesus spoke out against, like self-righteousness, and we haven't been known for how we love like Jesus loved. We've become known more for who we've excluded than for who we've embraced, more for what we're against than what we're for.

It's true that some of the loudest voices within Christianity haven't been the most beautiful voices, and some of the most beautiful voices of faith haven't been the loudest. The media has helped perpetuate these stereotypes at times by amplifying sick and absurd expressions of so-called Christianity marked by hatred, like the pastor in Florida who burned the Qur'an or the Westboro Baptist folks who hold "God hates fags" signs. Too often the haters have hijacked the headlines, and the stories of our faith that are so beautiful haven't gotten much airtime. But the blame doesn't rest on the media alone. It's as if they had a gun, and we gave them the bullets.

Evangelicals in particular have an image crisis, whether it's deserved or not. When people hear the word *evangelical*, it conjures up an image of folks who are antigay, antifeminist, antienvironment, proguns, prowar, and pro–capital punishment. We often look very unlike our Christ.

One does have to wonder whether the evangelicals of old who were so passionate about peace and caring for the poor and ending slavery would even recognize the evangelicalism of today. If John Wesley or William Wilberforce or Charles Finney were alive today, would they be evangelicals?

It's important to name something from the beginning. Evangelicalism, like many things in our society, has been shaped, defined, and dominated by white male culture. Even when you look at the Wikipedia page for *evangelicalism*, you see the faces and names of white men. It's hard to find any heroic women or people of color mentioned in the movement at all. And that is part of our problem.

Evangelicalism has been colonized. There are many women and men of all ethnicities who are by every definition evangelical, but they have been erased. Some of them were never invited onto the ship to begin with. And others were thrown off the ship because even though their theology aligned, their politics did not. And there are those who jumped ship voluntarily because they didn't want their faith to be colonized by a faith that was more white than Christlike. Many of the young evangelicals I know want nothing to do with the evangelical label or brand.

To be fair, the media have also contributed to the whitening of evangelicalism by seeing it as a voting bloc rather than as a religious bloc, defining it by political choices rather than theological convictions. They've helped perpetuate stereotypes by putting the spotlight on evangelical "spokesmen" who fit the conservative political pundit role, and they ignore the evangelicals who don't. So in addition to being colonized, evangelicalism also got hijacked. Even white evangelicals find themselves held hostage inside evangelicalism.

In a *USA Today* piece titled "Evangelicals Aren't Who You Think," my friend Jim Wallis pointed out that the term *evangelical* has been a victim of identity theft. Despite the fact that there are massive numbers of evangelicals of color—African American, Latino, Asian, native, young and old, women and men—the media continually erases these voices.[1]

Not only is it harmful to the silenced multitudes, it's also inaccurate reporting. The *USA Today* piece showed that while "evangelicals" were being shown overwhelmingly in support of Trump, it was actually "white evangelicals." Polls from LifeWay and Reuters showed that when all of evangelicalism is included, the percentage of Trump support drops dramatically, into a minority.[2] Jim Wallis is right; there has been an identity theft, and millions of people have been erased and misrepresented in the process. And Wallis is also right when he says, "If the mistaken perception persists that evangelicals overwhelmingly support Trump in this election, it could mean the obituary of the true meaning of 'evangelical' in America—especially for a new generation."[3]

Part of me hates to surrender the word *evangelical* to the folks who have hijacked it, stolen it, or colonized it, as it were. There are many black and brown Christian leaders who may not be willing to give up on the word or be ready to surrender the label. I hope to follow their lead as we consider the future of evangelicalism. Perhaps there is a new evangelicalism that rises from the compost of the old. As we approach the fiftieth anniversary of some of the definitive moments of modern evangelicalism, such as the Lausanne Conference of 1974 and the Chicago Declaration of 1973—which happened before I was born—perhaps it is time for a new summit, one where people of color represent a majority of the delegates as they listen to the Spirit and discern evangelicalism's future.

As for me, for the first time in my life, I'm not interested in fighting to take evangelicalism back from the folks who stole it. *Evangelical* is not the only label I've used—and maybe not even my preferred one. But it's also not one I've felt the need to distance myself from—until recently.

So I'm a bit indifferent. I like what evangelicalism has been in the past. I think our black and brown brothers and sisters and our international friends around the globe could very well take the brand and label back from the white minority that has monopolized and defiled it—if they want to.

Most of the young folks I meet couldn't care less about the word or have no idea what it means to begin with. So I've been ambivalent about its use as a label in recent years. I've used it when it's helpful and avoided it when it's not.

Admittedly, I'm a bit of a minimalist who likes self-identifying as simply a "follower of Jesus" or a "disciple of Christ." Even just "Christian" is good enough for me. I realize Christians don't always have the best reputation in the world, but I see that as a challenge to sing a better harmony rather than give up on the choir. That's why my preferred label these days is "red-letter Christian." (I'll say more about that later.)

Before I take a closer look at the future of evangelicalism, let me take a second to look back.

THE END OF AN ERA

It's nothing new for Christians to retire secondary labels that have hit their expiration date. Over the decades, some Christians have embraced various labels to distinguish themselves from other Christians whose beliefs they deem heretical or sometimes just disagreeable. During the late 1800s, there was a recasting of

Christianity in the wake of the rational and scientific age of modernity that became known as fundamentalism, so named because US and British scholars published a twelve-volume series called *The Fundamentals of the Christian Faith* that outlined doctrine in the early Christian creeds.

The fundamentalist label served many well until around 1930. But after the famous Scopes trial, in which William Jennings Bryan argued against Darwin's theory of evolution, many viewed fundamentalists as anti-intellectual, naive, and judgmental. Fundamentalism began to gain a reputation for its strict moral code, which included condemning things such as dancing, smoking, and the consumption of alcohol. As the old saying I heard growing up goes, "We don't drink, smoke, or chew—or date girls that do."

By the 1950s, the word *fundamentalist* was viewed so negatively that some wondered whether it could be redeemed. About that time, some Christians, including influential evangelist Billy Graham and the then-editor of *Christianity Today* magazine, Carl Henry, began using a new name: *evangelical*.

The word *evangelical* served us well until end of the 1900s. In the 1980s, the religious right began to align itself with the Republican National Committee. And things began to go haywire, as they do any time the church gets in bed with the empire.

THE FINAL HOORAH

By the mid-nineties, the word *evangelical* had developed the image problem we have today.

Of course, it all climaxed in this last election with the support for Trump—as 81 percent of white evangelicals supported him. This support came despite the fact that his actions and life choices contradict the core values that have been the bedrocks of evangelicalism itself—things such as not having multiple sexual partners, appearing on the cover of *Playboy*, or bragging about sexual assault.

At this point, it feels like evangelicalism and conservative politics have been put in a blender, so I'm not confident they can be separated from each other again. Ironically, many evangelicals—and white evangelical leaders in particular, so often known for their zeal for Jesus, commitment to family values, and pursuit of virtuous living—became infatuated with Trump. Many ended up talking more about him than about Jesus. If aliens from another planet listened in on this past election, they may have reasonably concluded that the Savior of white evangelicals is a man named Donald Trump rather than a man named Jesus.

This is what led to an uprising even at Jerry Falwell's Liberty University, the largest evangelical college in the country. Thousands of Liberty students spoke out against Trump as well as Falwell's support of him. At Liberty, we can see a clear example of the generational collision between the children of the culture wars, such as Jerry Falwell Jr., and the Christians of the next generation, who are increasingly frustrated with politics and are still in love with Jesus.

After Trump's first one hundred days in office, support from white evangelicals had soared to over 75 percent. And Jerry Falwell Jr. made this stunning statement: "I think evangelicals have found their dream president."[4]

Despite the outcry of students, Trump was invited again to Liberty, this time to give the commencement speech in May 2017. Perhaps most strikingly, he was invited to return even though he didn't mention Jesus a single time during his first speech at America's largest evangelical school. It was enough to talk about himself and his politics. If Jerry Falwell Jr. is correct that Donald Trump is the "dream president" of evangelicals, we are all in trouble. The gospel of Trump is very different from the gospel of Christ. The lifestyle of Trump is very different from the lifestyle prescribed in the Sermon on the Mount. Trump seems to better embody the seven deadly sins than the Beatitudes.

THE *OTHER* EVANGELICALS

Evangelical icons such as Max Lucado grieved the shocking support of Christians for Trump. Eighty evangelical leaders released "A Declaration of American Evangelicals Concerning Trump" that quickly jumped to over twenty thousand signatures. A group of hundreds of evangelical women released their own petition. The voices of dissent were legion, and one more is worth noting. Andy Crouch, executive editor of *Christianity Today*, had this to say in his eloquent article "Speak Truth to Trump":

> There is a point at which strategy becomes its own idolatry— an attempt to manipulate the levers of history in favor of the causes we support. . . . Enthusiasm for a candidate like Trump gives our neighbors ample reason to doubt that we believe Jesus is Lord. They see that some of us are so self-interested, and so self-protective, that we will ally ourselves with someone who violates all that is sacred to us.[5]

There are other prominent evangelical voices of dissent worth noting, such as Southern Baptist ethicist Russell Moore. He was a steady critic of Trump and just as much a critic of his fellow evangelicals who jumped on board the Trump train. He gave a powerful eulogy to the religious right at the prestigious Erasmus Lecture in October 2016. In that lecture, Moore said, "When Christianity is seen as a political project in search of a gospel useful enough to advance its worldly agenda, it will end up pleasing those who make politics primary, while losing those who believe the Gospel."[6] In other words, you can't serve two masters.

He ended the lecture by boldly naming the fact that "the Religious Right turns out to be the people the Religious Right warned us about"—namely, folks who forsake Jesus to support candidates that serve their own interests more than Christ's.[7]

It's been said that God created us in his image, and we decided to return the favor. It's the only way to explain how folks can claim to be Christian and support a man who contradicts nearly every one of the teachings of Jesus in the Sermon on the Mount, both in his policies and in his personal life.

Moore's speech sounded like a eulogy: "A Religious Right that is not able to tie public action and cultural concern to a theology of gospel and mission will die, and will deserve to die."[8] And he was the perfect person to write the eulogy to white evangelicalism. He is white, male, Southern Baptist, evangelical, conservative, a beloved child of the religious right—and now he is done with the word *evangelical*. He seemed to surrender the label *evangelical*, now preferring to call himself a "gospel-centered" Christian—or perhaps a red-letter Christian.

It's important to be clear that what has died, or is on its deathbed, is not evangelicalism, but *white* evangelicalism. I am still optimistic that the unhealthiest voices within evangelicalism are aging out and not producing many young charismatic leaders. John Hagee, James Dobson, Ralph Reed, Jerry Falwell,

Pat Robertson—these are the old-guard white evangelicals. As Moore put it: "There are no twenty-two-year-old John Hagees."[9] (If you don't know who Hagee is, don't worry. That's the point.)

It's worth noting that some of these older voices, such as James Dobson and Wayne Grudem, were less enthusiastic this past election—some even retracted their initial support. And several significant older white evangelical leaders deviated from the overwhelming support of Trump among the evangelical tribe. Nonetheless, 81 percent is a lot. One can't help but think that more risks could have been taken. And the collateral damage of this support when it comes to the integrity of the Christian witness could be massive and catastrophic.

The evangelicalism that is growing is the more beautiful versions of it—both around the world and even here in the United States. What's in question is whether these new evangelicals will want anything to do with the brand. After all, the same people who led many of us to Jesus have now led us to Trump.

Those of the new generation—whether it wants to be called evangelical or not—love Jesus and care about justice. They care about life—the earth, the poor, refugees, and immigrants. They know that black lives matter and that racism is real. For them, a consistent ethic of life shapes the way they think about war and militarism, gun violence and police brutality, the death penalty and mass incarceration. Being pro-life doesn't just mean being antiabortion; it is about being *for life*. And an inconsistent ethic of life has caused many postevangelicals to jump ship.

It's clear that when it comes to religion in America, the fastest growing groups are the "nones" (nonaffiliated), ex-Catholics, and recovering evangelicals—and one reason is that they see the contradictions of white evangelicalism so clearly.

INTENSIVE CARE

If evangelicalism is to survive the current crisis, I suggest it will require at least three radical shifts: a consistent ethic of life, authenticity, and a renewed focus on Jesus.

Too often *pro-life* has come to mean probirth or antiabortion, as if abortion were the only *life* issue. Wouldn't it be beautiful to have a pro-life movement that stands against abortion but also stands just as passionately against the death penalty, gun violence, militarism and war, the degradation of creation, police brutality, and all other things that destroy life? That would truly be a pro-life movement. Being pro-life is not only about protecting the unborn but also about supporting folks after they are born.

In a world filled with violence, one of the most important things we can talk about today is the need for a consistent ethic of life. I like to say that I'm pro-life from the womb to the tomb.

Every human being is made in the image of God, and any time a life is lost, we lose a little glimpse of God in the world. For evangelicalism to recover from the contradictions it has become known for, it will need a consistent life ethic. The language of that ethic, the seamless garment, has been a helpful ethical framework for many people over the centuries. Early Christians stood consistently against all killing, speaking passionately against abortion, the death penalty, murder, and war. And today a consistent life ethic is resonating with a new generation of evangelicals, especially young folks.

We are tired of death. We also are tired of a two-party system because neither the Democrats nor the Republicans has a consistent ethic of life. Many Republicans are against abortion. Many Democrats are against gun violence. But *both parties* promise to increase military spending. It creates a quagmire for those of us who are tired of death and for whom a value for life is our ethical framework.

All of us who seek to be pro-life should continue to care about abortion, but we should just as passionately care about the death penalty, gun violence, the movement for black lives, the crisis of refugees and immigrants, the environment, health care, mass incarceration, and all the other issues that are destroying the lives and squashing the dignity of children whom God created and loves so deeply.

We also need authenticity. For too long, evangelicalism has been defined by beliefs rather than by practices, by doctrines rather than by actions. When we focus on beliefs alone, we end up with great theologians, televangelists, and preachers. When we focus on lifestyle Christianity, we produce saints. That's what we need today—not just more preachers, but also some saints.

We can maintain our orthodoxy (right thinking) while reclaiming our orthopraxis (right living). Doctrinal statements are important things, but they are hard things to love. God didn't just give us words on paper; the Word became flesh. And now we are to put flesh on our faith. In the end, Christianity spreads best not by force but by fascination. And the last few decades of evangelicalism have become less and less fascinating. We've had much to say with our mouths but often very little to show from our lives. People can't hear what we say, because our hypocrisies are too loud.

That's what I love about Mother Teresa. She's been one of my mentors. She used to say, "Our best sermon is our life." She didn't just say she was pro-life; she showed us she was pro-life. She took in fourteen-year-old moms and picked up orphans abandoned in the train stations of Calcutta.

I had the privilege of working with her in India. While I was there, I learned that some folks called her "Mother Teresa" because she truly was their mother. She had raised them.

I remember meeting a young man, about thirty years old, who said to me, "You know why we call her Mother Teresa, right?" I shook my head curiously. He went on, "Because she's our mom." He showed me things she had given him over the years, just as any mom would give her kids. That's the sort of integrity that the pro-life movement needs today.

I want to be pro-life like Mother Teresa was pro-life—and that means taking in teenage mothers and walking alongside families in poverty. It means creating support groups for people who have chosen to have abortions and are living with the pain of that decision. It means getting involved in the lives of folks facing execution and standing against all killing, both legal and illegal.

Mother Teresa didn't just picket abortion clinics. She didn't just have T-shirts and a bumper sticker reading, "Abortion is murder." She raised young people. If we are truly pro-life, we had better have some teen moms and foster kids living in our homes.

And Mother Teresa knew that abortion was not the only life issue. She was just as passionately against the death penalty and made some personal phone calls to governors in the United States to stop executions. She told them, "Do what Jesus would do." She even wrote a letter to John Dear, who was in a North Carolina jail for protesting war, and asked him to proclaim the love of Jesus to the poor in prison.

Mother Teresa consistently spoke out courageously for life. She's a great model for us today as we seek to be pro-life—not just in word but also in deed.

So let us reimagine the pro-life movement today as a movement that stands consistently for life and against death. And let us move beyond stale rhetoric and ideologies to action.

RISING FROM THE COMPOST OF CHRISTENDOM

This toxicity within evangelicalism runs so deep we are left with few options. One is to attempt to take back the term *evangelical* from the older white folks who have hijacked it. It will not be long before they're the minority within evangelicalism. It is clear that some of the loudest voices have not been the healthiest voices when it comes to representing Christ in the world. And some of the beautiful voices have been silenced, squashed, or marginalized.

We can amplify the voices of "the other evangelicals," the young, black, brown, Asian, Native evangelicals who are quickly becoming the majority of evangelicalism though they aren't the loudest voices out there and though the media seems to find it impossible to admit their existence. We can point out that the root of *evangelicalism* means "the good news," even though much of what evangelicalism has come to represent is anything but good news. We can point out the great revivalists who, like Charles Finney, had two motivations when they gave their famous altar calls: to invite people not only to dedicate their lives to Jesus but also to sign up for the movement to abolish slavery. That's what evangelicalism *was*. So that's one option, and frankly, it seems like a preferable, albeit very daunting, one. We can't continue to allow the "other" evangelical friends to be erased and silenced.

The second option is to create something new. Gandhi spoke of building a "new world in the shell of the old one." What we have in mind is precisely that: building a new Christianity in the shell of the old one. Just as new life can rise from stinky compost, so can new life arise from the compost of Christendom.

Last year, the world lost a wonderful woman named Phyllis Tickle, a very influential Christian leader and writer. One of the things she mentioned often is that the church needs a rummage sale every few hundred years. We have to get rid of the clutter, discover forgotten treasures, and dust off the family heirlooms. We've just crossed the five-hundredth anniversary of the Reformation. Perhaps it's time for another rummage sale, a new reformation.

For decades, many of us have tried to reclaim the label *evangelical*, pointing out that its roots predate Jesus and that means "proclaimer of good news." Interestingly enough, it was an imperial word that was ripped out of the political lexicon of Rome and used subversively by Jesus and the early Christians.

To be clear, we are clinging to the gospel as we denounce what evangelicalism has come to mean. I do not want to be the collateral damage of white evangelicalism. I'm skeptical after this last election season that *evangelical* is a word that we can redeem. But I will never abandon the evangel—the gospel. It is the gospel and our Savior Jesus that compel me to denounce what evangelicalism has become in North America. I cling to the gospel that many of my fellow evangelicals have abandoned.

The interesting thing is that many have turned from institutional Christianity and from evangelicalism for the same reason: these groups forgot their foundations. They've gotten distracted from Jesus. Lots of folks like Jesus; they just aren't crazy about Christians.

As cliché as it may sound, the only hope for Christianity— and for evangelicalism—is Jesus.

A NEW ALTAR CALL

When we lose Christ as the cornerstone, everything else is on shaky ground. Our brother Rev. William Barber, who has been a prophetic voice in this season, often says, "When we stop focusing on Jesus, we end up talking a lot about things Jesus didn't talk much about, and we don't talk about the things Jesus had a whole lot to say about."

Jesus must be the foundation for all our political convictions. He is the lens through which we understand the world and the Bible. There's an old hymn that goes like this: "My hope is built on nothing less than Jesus' blood and righteousness. . . . On Christ the solid rock I stand, all other ground is sinking sand." Over the centuries, Christians, at their best, have refused to place their hope in anything short of Jesus. After all, the word *vote* shares the same root as *devotion* and has everything to do with where we rest our hope and where our loyalty lies. Our devotion to Jesus and the "least of these" creates the framework for how we think about every issue, whether it is immigration, capital punishment, abortion, or health care.

We hear a lot about God blessing America, but the Bible doesn't say, "God so loved America." It says, "God so loved the world." And in the Sermon on the Mount, Jesus named those that God especially blesses: the poor, the meek, the merciful, those who mourn, the pure in heart, the peacemakers. God seems to bless the very antithesis of many of the things America has come to stand for: prosperity, pride, and power. The prophets of old would undoubtedly call it idolatry. We have made idols out of wealth, fame, power, and whiteness, and the phenomena of Trump is a natural outgrowth of that idolatry.

The things Jesus said couldn't be more relevant to the world we live in.

And the things Jesus said stand in stark contrast to many of the things America has come to adore.

I believe it was the legendary Wendell Berry, farmer and theologian, who once quipped about how our money says "In God We Trust," but our economy looks like the seven deadly sins. When those sins, which include greed, lust, and vanity, have become credentials for our country's highest office, we are all in trouble, especially if the prophetic conscience of the church surrenders her voice to these cultural idols.

Donald Trump is only a man. But the movement behind him unveils an idolatry that has intoxicated many of our fellow Christians.

The words of Jesus stand in contrast to the world we live in. "Sell your possessions and give to the poor" doesn't win many friends on Wall Street (Matthew 19:21). "Whoever finds their life will lose it" sounds a lot different from the gospel of the Kardashians (Matthew 10:39). "Love your enemies" (Matthew 5:44) is a tough command in a world of ISIS or in a world that feeds you to beasts in an arena and hangs you upside down on crosses. But alas, those of us who choose to follow Christ over the empire must count the cost.

It is nothing new for Christianity to get polluted by the world around us and forget who we are meant to be. When asked about Jesus, Mahatma Gandhi remarked that he loved Jesus but wished the Christians took him seriously. Too often we look very unlike our Christ. No one knows that better than Africans who came to America at the hands of white "Christians" or Native Americans who were mercilessly killed by white "Christians."

The words of Frederick Douglass ring true today:

> Between the Christianity of this land, and the Christianity
> of Christ, I recognize the widest possible difference—
> so wide, that to receive the one as good, pure, and holy is
> of necessity to reject the other as bad, corrupt, and wicked.
> . . . I love the pure, peaceable, and impartial Christianity
> of Christ; I therefore hate the corrupt, slaveholding,
> women-whipping, cradle-plundering, partial and hypo-
> critical Christianity of this land. Indeed, I can see no
> reason, but the most deceitful one, for calling the religion
> of this land Christianity.[10]

The amazing thing is that Jesus has survived the embarrassing things we Christians have done in his name. So
perhaps this is a moment for evangelicals to repent and be
born again—again.

Here's the good news. There is a home for homeless Christians. And there is a safe place to explore Christianity for folks
who aren't quite ready to give up on Jesus.

There is a movement of red-letter Christians—those who
want a Christianity that looks like Jesus. It all started with a
radio host in Nashville, Tennessee. He was interviewing a
friend of mine, Jim Wallis, on the radio, and the DJ didn't seem
to have too much to do with Christianity. He mentioned having
read most of the Bible. There were parts he really liked, and
other parts he found confusing. But then he said something
interesting. Referring to the old Bibles that have the words of
Jesus highlighted in red, he said, "I've always like the stuff in
red. You all seem to like the stuff in red. You should call your-
selves red-letter Christians." And it stuck.

Here's our pledge:

I dedicate my life to Jesus, and commit to live as if Jesus meant the things he said in the "red letters" of Scripture.

I will allow Jesus and his teaching to shape my decisions and priorities.

I denounce belief-only Christianity and refuse to allow my faith to be a ticket into heaven and an excuse to ignore the suffering world around me.

I will seek first the kingdom of God—on earth as it is in heaven—and live in a way that moves the world toward God's dream, where the first are last and the last are first, where the poor are blessed and the peacemakers are the children of God, working toward a society where all are treated equally and resources shared equitably.

I recognize that I will fall short in my attempts to follow Jesus, and I trust in God's grace and the community to catch me when I do.

I know that I cannot do this alone, so I commit to share this journey with others who are walking in the way of Jesus. I will surround myself with people who remind me of Jesus, help me become more like him, and hold me accountable for my actions and words.

I will share Jesus with the world, with my words and with my deeds. Like Jesus, I will interrupt injustice and stand up for the life and dignity of all. I will allow my life to point toward Christ, everywhere I go.

Let's live like Jesus really meant the stuff he said. Let's imagine a Christianity that looks like Jesus again, a faith worth believing in, an evangelicalism that's known for love again. And then let's build the church.

10

THE IMPORTANCE OF LISTENING
IN TODAY'S EVANGELICALISM

JIM DALY

t's natural that with the passage of time, things change. It's
every bit as reliable as death and taxes. For good and bad, this
has been true of evangelicalism. What follows is my perspective
from over twenty-five years in a parachurch ministry. While the
evangelical message hasn't changed—we are collectively committed to the faithful proclamation of the great news of Jesus
Christ—both our approach to that message and the makeup of
our community have changed in important ways.

First, whether we think it good or not, evangelicalism is an
increasingly personality-driven movement. We often mark its
founding and development by mentioning *names* rather than
events or theological and ecclesiastical developments. We collectively know what these key names represent in the growth and
influence of our movement: D. L. Moody, Dawson Trotman, Billy
Graham, Bill Bright, Jerry Falwell, Francis Schaeffer, John Stott,
James Kennedy, Chuck Colson, Chuck Swindoll, and James

Dobson, to name just a few. Most of these men were (or are) larger-than-life figures, although that was not their intention at all. They became institutions in their own right.

This isn't as true of most evangelical leaders today. We certainly have large personalities and influence, but not to the degree of our forefathers. Compare Jerry Falwell to his son, Jerry Falwell Jr. Or contrast Bill Bright with Cru's current president, Steve Douglass. The second-generation leaders are certainly highly effective, perhaps even more than their predecessors in some ways. But their personalities are not as closely tied to the organizations they lead.

This has been true in my experience as well. Dr. James Dobson was an extremely talented and charismatic mental health professional with a solid academic pedigree when he founded Focus on the Family. I arrived at the ministry as a paper salesman for a multinational corporation. I came up through the ranks over the years, and no one was more stunned than I when I was chosen to take over Dobson's leadership. Of course, I had some skill at running an organization, and I knew what Focus on the Family's mission was and how to accomplish it. But no one knew who I was. I was not a personality. That is a role I had to grow into to some degree, and it has been one of the greatest challenges of my job. I think the same is true for others who have stepped in to fill leadership roles held by evangelical icons.

This shift from iconic personalities to numerous lesser-knowns has to do with two things, I think. One is the ways our culture has shifted in its appraisal of authority and influence. We no longer place a premium on personality and reputation. The lab-coated individual in advertisements is a rarity today. It's true that we do afford no small measure of fame to certain preachers and authors, but this grouping seems to be more diverse today than in centuries past. And few of these leaders dominate the pack like leaders in earlier decades.

This is largely due to a second change: the diversification of media outlets and opportunities. To the surprise and frustration of old media, we now have a vast array of platforms for new voices beyond radio, books, and television. Self-publishing, podcasting, and blogging have democratized communication—including the sharing of the gospel. Although not without its perils, this is a very good development for the church. It puts the power of Gutenberg and Marconi in the hands of everyone and broadens the field of influential voices. Bloggers and podcasters can now have a tremendous impact on the church and society at large—more than many radio Bible teachers of yesteryear—and they don't even have to leave their house. The whole game has changed.

While some institutions of evangelicalism are speaking to smaller audiences, there are more voices speaking to *growing* audiences. This means the average believer has access to more precise and parochial information. We have the "restless and reformed" in the Gospel Coalition/John Piper/Tim Keller community. We have a tidal wave of smart mom bloggers. We have creative young adults in the *Relevant* magazine camp. This free flow of information and ideas makes for a stronger, more robust evangelical community.

I often reflect on how our transition in leadership here at Focus on the Family denotes these generational changes in very personal ways. Dr. Dobson had an idyllic childhood. He was the only child of James, a faithful pastor and father, and Myrtle, a doting, homemaking mother. He grew up under the security of their boundless love, their enduring marriage, and their attentive and principled parenting. In fact, his lineage provided him with a deep and godly heritage. This experience served as an effective launching pad for James Dobson Jr. as he launched what would become the world-changing ministry known as Focus on the Family.

My story could not be more different. My parents divorced when I was very young. My mom died of cancer when I was nine. My dad drank himself to death by the time I was twelve. I was an orphan before I even got out of elementary school. I spent time in the foster care system. The stability and love of an intact Christian home—the very things that informed Dobson's experience—were foreign to me. My passion for thriving, stable families stems from that vacuum in my childhood.

While there has never been a golden age of the family—the impact of the fall is felt across every generation—the one that produced Dobson came pretty close. But the world into which he emerged was changing drastically. His first book, *Dare to Discipline*, was his response to an increasingly permissive society that celebrated individuality and self-expression as the highest good, even in children. He was the "anti-Dr. Spock" and proudly so. His meteoric rise in popularity demonstrated how many parents desired this type of back-to-basics approach. He became one of the most trusted parenting guides in the United States, if not the world.

As his career grew, Dobson started involving himself in the public square and public policy. He was deeply concerned with how quickly the traditional values of the world in which he grew up were disappearing. He was committed to staunching this moral hemorrhage, even at the expense of his reputation. Many of his leading peers in evangelicalism saw the world the same way. Preserving what was being lost became the primary fuel propelling the so-called religious right.

My childhood and formative years, like those of so many of my peers, took place in a very different setting. We grew up as victims of this cultural slide. We have little, if any, memory of "the good old days." There was little we sought to preserve, having grown up in the midst of the sexual, humanistic, and agnostic/New Age revolutions. The divorce rate started to rocket in the years of our adolescence and didn't slow down until we reached our thirties.

Intact, lifelong marriages and families were unknown to many of us, in our own homes and in those of our friends. They were like UFOs or Bigfoot. We had heard stories and seen grainy photos, but mostly we doubted they existed. But we would have loved to have seen one! We were the latchkey generation because so few of our moms were home at the end of the school day. We faced an increasingly toxic media culture, with illicit drugs and pornography becoming commonplace. All of this marked us deeply. Dobson and the leaders of his generation were right to call it out.

For us, there was little to look back on with warm feelings. All we had in front of us was an uncertain future. It was up to us to help shape it into something positive. One generation looked back longingly. Ours had no option but to look forward hopefully.

It's a sociological truism that every generation's view of life and the world, its work ethic, and its heartfelt desires, values, and dreams are largely shaped by what preceded it. The children of the Great Depression grew to be the most prosperous and steady our nation has ever seen. Their children became the anti-establishment, antimaterialist flower children, but they grew up to be the yuppies of the Reagan years. And their children became the Gen Xers who brought in the technological revolution.

Gen Xers and their younger millennial peers dearly yearn for the family stability of earlier decades. They might be all for "family diversity" in theory, but nearly every poll in which they participate shows that lifelong marriage and parenthood are their primary goals. They want to create a very different family culture from the one in which they were raised. This fact significantly shapes this generation—the largest our nation has ever seen. And it impacts how we approach our mission at Focus on the Family.

It's interesting to think about these generational changes in terms of the archetypes of prophet and evangelist. James Dobson fits the mold of a prophet, calling millions around the world to stand firm in what he often referred to as "the campaign for righteousness." My wiring is more toward the evangelism side of the equation. I'm passionate in my belief that the gospel changes individuals, families, and communities.

This has impacted Focus on the Family's approach to certain hot-button issues. As we continue to push back against a culture of abortion in favor of a culture of life, it has been very important to me to reach across the aisle and engage those with whom we disagree. Representatives of Planned Parenthood and NARAL have said that they want abortion to be "safe, legal, and rare." Obviously, as a pro-life ministry, we can't agree that abortion is ever safe. And we certainly hope for a day when *Roe v. Wade* will be overturned. But in the meantime, I think it's important to sit down with our ideological opponents and say, "You want abortion to be rare. How can we work together to make that happen?"

As pro-life evangelicals, we might not be able to end abortion outright, but how many babies might be saved in the short term if we would be willing to find areas we can agree on with those with whom we disagree?

I feel a similar burden to find opportunities where we can engage the issues related to gender and sexuality. We are to bring God's peace into the world's chaos. As we endeavor to be faithful in both truth and grace, it has been my desire to put a human face on those we oppose. When I first assumed the role of president of Focus on the Family, I kept a small scrap of paper on my desk with a phone number on it. The number was for a prominent and well-connected LGBTQ activist. I finally called him, and to my surprise, he was willing to meet with me. We've since built a solid friendship.

As evangelicals engage the world (for that is our full orientation—taking the good news of the gospel of Christ to those outside the church and into the public square), we must remember that no group is monolithic. Just as we don't care for it when people view all Christians as a caricature, we should understand that "the world" isn't monolithic either. Not all atheists are angry with the church and want to steal away our children. Not all college professors and media professionals are "humanists," out to attack Christianity at every turn. Not everyone outside our community hates Christians or dislikes our engagement in the culture. Not even most.

Of course, some individuals and groups are strongly opposed to what we stand for, and we should be mindful and ready to counter them in truth and love as we meet them. But not everyone is like that, just as not all Christians are exactly like you or me. In fact, think about this: the body of Christ is the most diverse collection of people on the planet, probably more so than any other group. This is God's design. It makes his church both attractive and influential.

Rather than assuming what "those people" are like, we should get to know them. It's much easier than we might imagine. Each person we meet is an individual created by God, unique as any snowflake. We should embrace people in their uniqueness and be not only willing but *eager* to talk to them and ask them about their beliefs, their stories, and what makes them who they are. I believe we should have two questions on the tip of our tongue as we engage with those around us:

1. Help me understand what you believe.

2. What brought you to those conclusions?

This requires being good listeners. People who met Pope John Paul II throughout his life remarked about what an intense listener he was. Nothing else existed when he engaged with someone. The person in front of him was always the most important thing going on at the moment. He wanted to experience that person and discover who she was as a unique God-imager. As evangelicals, we would do well to adopt this same perspective.

John Stott talked about the importance of evangelicals being good listeners better and more profoundly than anyone I know. He once wrote, "Bad listeners do not make good disciples."[1] And the apostle James entreats us, "My dear brothers and sisters, take note of this: Everyone should be quick to listen, slow to speak, and slow to become angry" (James 1:19).

Stott proposed that evangelicals must be listeners in three distinct ways: listeners to God, listeners to others, and listeners to the world. Let me explain what he means by these.

Listenering to God. This should be basic, but it's easier said than done. It takes an investment of time to sit quietly with God and let him speak to us. Often he doesn't seem to be in a hurry. Neither should we. We may feel as if God is saying something to us after a period of time, putting a message or impression on our hearts. But it's important to sit quietly with that and continue to listen. Often our richest experiences with the Lord come after a sacrifice of *time.* We do well to sit at the Master's feet, as Mary of Bethany did, listening intently without feeling rushed by the things that need doing. What could be more important than hearing and then responding to his words to us?

Listening to others. Stott calls this "double listening": listening to God and then listening intently to others. Only in careful and intentional listening can we meet the needs of others. Their need may be to hear the message of salvation, or it may be for practical help or a word of encouragement or correction. God has put it on my heart to listen in this way with some of the people I encounter "across the aisle" on issues such as the sanctity of life and sexuality. I have felt burdened to just pick up the phone and get to know them, or to meet for coffee or a meal the next time I'm in their town.

Why do they feel or believe the way they do, and how did they arrive there? What is the life story that made them the people they are? What are their most important hopes, dreams, fears, and struggles? I ask with sincerity how our team at Focus on the Family and I might pray for them. In many ways, the simplest way we love others is just *listening* to them with interest and without rush, and for no other reason than just to hear them. Genuine listening is not a means to our ends.

Listening to the world. The famous sons of Issachar understood the times and provided insight into what Israel should do (1 Chronicles 12). Their understanding came from listening carefully and discerningly to the world. In the same way, we should pay attention to the culture around us and become students of it. Billy Graham was a master of this in his day, and it shaped his preaching in colorful ways.

What are people talking about? What concerns them, and what occupies their time, money, and attention? What's happening politically in the world? What's driving cultural trends and developments? Seeing the bigger picture often starts with the second kind of listening: hearing personally from those who hold various and emerging views.

Being a good listener is a basic act of service and humility. It honors the dignity of the individual. People aren't offended or put off when someone is attentive to what they have to say. We gain and grow not be displaying what we know but by listening well to what others have to say and considering what they can teach us.

I would add that we need to be very attentive listeners to the past. There's so much we can learn from the heritage that we evangelicals have been given, not just by leaders of the last few decades or centuries but by leaders throughout the history of Christianity. We can learn from what they faithfully did right as well as from the mistakes they made. We must apply these insights and traditions to our present day and carry them into the future as we engage it with the experience, insight, and correction that God has given us in the midst of our generation. We must be like David, who faithfully "served the purpose of God in his own generation" (Acts 13:36 ESV). God calls each of us to a particular generation with its own unique challenges, opportunities, and possibilities. This generation is the stage on which he has called us to play a part in his story of redemption, with a mind toward what it will leave for the coming generation.

The future of evangelicalism rests ultimately with God, but he has chosen, through his great wisdom and mercy, to trust us with its care. We have a duty to serve this purpose faithfully and to train the next generation to do the same within the context of its own unique and changing times.

The consequences of our success or failure are great indeed.

11

HOPE FOR THE NEXT GENERATION

TOM LIN

While searching for an image that captures my assessment of and hopes for evangelicalism, I recall a rocky hilltop in northeast Ethiopia. It was isolated, rising a distance from a university town. As I climbed to the top, the view was a barren moonscape of browns and beiges punctuated only by rocks and debris. Absent were any signs of vegetation or shelter. The sun had baked away water and life from that land long ago. I shut my eyes in its harsh light as it relentlessly revealed every crack and fissure in the ground. The breeze, blowing as it will, brought no relief from the 105-degree heat. It dried my mouth, making me reluctant to speak.

JUST A PILE OF ROCKS?

That hilltop reminds me of American evangelicalism. For all of its size and statements about cultural engagement, it remains relatively distant from the centers of intellectual and cultural life. For all of its announcements and activity, it can seem arid and lifeless.

As the leader of a ministry to university students and faculty, I regularly hear the reasons younger generations reject our evangelical faith. They despise our ongoing tolerance of or complicity in racism, sexism, jingoism, and homophobia. They are disgusted by how we jockey for power and discouraged by the slight difference faith makes in our behavior. I could go on, but other contributors to this volume will more thoroughly identify our failures and flaws. However, in short, students and faculty see our sin and our hypocrisy, and they abhor it.

I see it as well and want to shut my eyes. I understand why many who share evangelical theological commitments are reluctant to speak or have considered abandoning the term and the identity as meaningless.[1] But I still have hope for evangelicalism.

From a certain angle at that hilltop, one could discern that many of the rocks have been arranged in casual rows. The rows face a cairn. It's just wide enough to hold a small Bible. University students who are a part of Evangelical Students' Union of Ethiopia (EvaSUE), a local Ethiopian campus ministry, call this hilltop Rock Chapel. They joyfully gather there several times each week to hear Scripture taught, to pray for their unsaved friends, and to worship our triune God.

Why meet there? The university prohibits them from meeting on campus. While it has offered a meeting space in a town several miles away, the students can't afford the bus fare to the other location, and they would be unable to bring their unsaved friends that far. So they meet at Rock Chapel, using rocks as their seats and rock as their pulpit. Their faithful presence transforms this wasteland into a chapel.

As we look at the context of American evangelicalism today, with its full array of complex challenges, these Ethiopian students give us hope.

To many, I'm part of a demographic that points to a brighter evangelical future—an ethnic minority who grew up in a fast-growing immigrant church, with a broad purview and access to significant resources to influence evangelicalism. As president of InterVarsity, trustee of Fuller Seminary, and trustee in the Lausanne Movement, I see the development of the next generation and the unceasing commitment to share the good news of the gospel. And as a trustee of a generous evangelical foundation, I see the funding of new wineskins—as well as the defunding of old wineskins—within evangelicalism. Through many lenses, I see hope for the future of evangelicalism and reasons to be encouraged.

EVANGELICALISM AS A GLOBAL FELLOWSHIP

The faithful witness of Ethiopian students reminds us that any evaluation of the word *evangelical* or *evangelicalism* must be done in the context of the global church. The decision of some American evangelicals to abandon the term is insensitive to our overseas sisters and brothers; it reflects the worst impulses of American exceptionalism and self-absorption. We have long since passed the era when American evangelicals may act independently. Even a cursory look at the global church provides great hope for the future of evangelicalism.

Global evangelicalism is growing in size and maturity. The vast majority of evangelicals live outside the United States, and their numbers are growing far faster than ours. Majority World evangelical theologians and biblical scholars, nurtured in part by ministries such as the Langham Partnership Scholars Program and Overseas Council, have reached a critical mass. They are no longer dependent on Western seminaries for degrees or Western publishers for translated or imported books. Theological and discipleship texts are now being written by and for their own contexts. Massive texts such as *The African Bible Commentary*[2] and *The South Asian Bible Commentary*[3] demonstrate the growing depth and breadth of the contextual theology they produce.

For American evangelicals, this should create humility to listen to and to learn from our sisters and brothers in the Majority World. We need to be discipled by them, even if we consider their integrative gospel too liberal or their theological positions too conservative. Because we American evangelicals are compromised by our underdeveloped political theology, we have much to learn about how to be disciples and citizens in pluralistic environments where power and privilege are lacking. We also have much to learn about reconciliation and justice from fellow believers who wrestle daily with the aftermath of genocide and ethnic cleaning.

Listening humbly and responsively to global voices will discipline us to be more attentive to those who are marginalized in our own country. In theology, biblical studies, mission, cultural engagement, and worship, the global church can give us tools to break free from a Christianity that resembles too closely the cultural priorities of the West,[4] answering the critiques of our harshest critics, both internally and externally.[5]

Global evangelicalism has become a full partner in world mission. Increasingly, Majority World Christians lead organizations that shape and define global evangelicalism (for example, IFES, OMF International, The Navigators, World Evangelical Alliance). Churches from the Majority World are already sending the majority of missionaries in the world today.[6] Global missions is polycentric—everyone to everywhere.

This is good news for American evangelicalism. We're moving increasingly from patronage relationships to true partnerships.[7] This is freeing us from latent imperialism, which has sadly shaped some of our missionary endeavors (both overseas and domestically). We're learning to engage in racial justice conversations that transcend the black/white duality and more fully reflect the breadth of our diverse society. It's changing the inherently consumerist mentality that drives so much ministry competition and creates wasteful duplications of efforts. It's teaching us to live more like the body of Christ and less like the shopping mall of Christ.

Mark Slaughter, an InterVarsity evangelist and the national facilitator for emerging generations for the US Lausanne movement, recently told participants at an international gathering that he had come to rely on the expertise of Majority World brothers and sisters. A fellow participant reacted with both shock and pleasure: "It's surprising and refreshing to find an American who thinks of himself as a learner rather than a teacher."

Global evangelicalism inspires us in the midst of our American malaise. I was recently with a university movement in Nigeria, where students worshiped passionately and with great hope. Security forces guarded the conference center with machine guns placed on the plenary stage; a terrorist attack was possible at any moment. Militant Islam is their top challenge. Students have lost loved ones to Boko Haram attacks, and 1.5 million have been forced from their homes in the Muslim north. However, these students are resilient in the midst of constant threat—not giving in to fear but boldly proclaiming the gospel wherever God leads them. Thousands at the conference responded to a call to move north intentionally, saying, "We won't give in to fear. The gospel is worth sacrificing our lives."

Their theological maturity and evangelistic fervor were inspiring. They considered present sufferings as nothing compared to "the souls of friends who suffer from not knowing the love of Christ." There was a standing ovation the last night when a speaker challenged all the Nigerians to go to China for their postgraduate studies. The students saw this as a wonderful opportunity to study abroad as mission, living out their vision to reach not only Chinese students but also more than four hundred thousand international students in that nation. It made me wonder, *How can we develop greater resiliency and passion for the gospel among American evangelical students?*

We have so much to learn from the global church. It may very well hold the keys to revival in the American evangelical church.

EVANGELICALISM AS A REFORM MOVEMENT

While we evangelicals like to demonstrate the continuity of our beliefs with the early church,[8] it's equally important to recognize how evangelicalism grows out of historic reform and revival movements.[9] According to British historian David Bebbington, these reform/revival movements shaped the four theological emphases that define evangelicalism today and have been widely accepted for several decades: biblicism, crucicentrism, conversionism, and activism.[10] The values and commitments of the Ethiopian students at Rock Chapel reflect these values. Just as these emphases brought reform and revival in the past, they hold the key to future reform and revival in American evangelicalism.

Biblicism. We believe in Scripture's power and authority. God speaks through his Word to change lives, change minds, and change the church. Therefore, we study it, memorize it, and (at our best) submit to it. When we do, God uses it to critique and affirm, reform and redirect our attitudes, beliefs, and behaviors.[11] When confronted by the clear teaching of Scriptures, we move to embrace change. Hence, Harold Ockenga's vision for evangelicalism in 1957 still resonates today:

> [Evangelicalism is] grounded upon the acceptance of the Bible as the Word of God, as plenarily inspired, and authoritative and infallible. Now on the basis of that Bible ... there is an application of this to the problems of the day, so that our view of God, and of man, and of the church, and of society, and of sin, and of salvation, must have its effects upon the social problems of the day.[12]

This is certainly true in campus ministry. Students confront injustice and confess sin because Scripture requires it. They extend forgiveness and expand friendship networks. They go overseas or return home.

This is also true for the church. The Presbyterian Church of America and the Southern Baptist Convention, two denominations whose histories have long been intertwined with racism, have made public confessions of their racial sins after being convicted by Scripture. While many of us wish students or denominational structures would change faster, we recognize that God uses his Word to convict and empower. This change didn't come because a multitude posted their displeasure or desires for reform on Twitter or Facebook. Rather, biblicism creates the possibility of reform and renewal.

Crucicentrism. We believe in the centrality of the cross as the place where God saves sinners, reveals himself, and conquers evil.[13] At the cross, we acknowledge the reality of our sin. We see God's love, mercy, holiness, and wrath. We celebrate his triumph over the powers of evil through Jesus' obedience and self-sacrifice. If Scripture confronts our hypocrisy, self-righteousness, sinfulness, and shamefulness, then the cross shows us how (and why) to respond. Convinced of our fallenness, we confess. Aware of God's holiness and wrath and comforted by his love and mercy, we repent. Confident that he can lift us above principalities and powers "by the blood of the Lamb" (Revelation 12:11), we witness in our weakness. So much of what many find distasteful in evangelicals would be cured if we simply clung to the cross.

Imagine if we enabled Christ's work on the cross to introduce a new radical standard of unity and reconciliation in the midst of our deeply divided church today. Imagine if we invested time and resources spreading the narrative of the cross outside the church, instead of time and resources spreading narratives that polarize us within the church. Imagine if we filled stadiums for public confession rather than for pop-culture worship. Imagine if we used social media to say, "I was wrong," rather than "you are wrong." Imagine if we cited our failures as freely as our faith.[14] The church expressed this type of behavior historically during times of revival. Those times could exist again. The cross shows us how.

Paul reminds us that the cross is a stumbling block (1 Corinthians 1:23). The cross challenges our pride, our self-sufficiency, our self-satisfaction, and our sin. A commitment to suffering and death to self is an anathema in today's platform culture, where evangelicals spend overwhelming resources to create sexy branding and visibility for their cause but take insufficient time to do the unsexy work of calling others to the cross. We are called not to build platforms but to be willing to submit to Jesus' platform, which is the cross. It is no surprise that cross-shaped evangelicalism faces a lack of approbation within the wider church and culture. We are not to seek triumphalism but the suffering servant on the cross.

Conversionism. We believe that God changes lives. He redeems rebels and sanctifies saints. This is a critical reminder. Many in our culture wish to say farewell to evangelicalism because the evangelical community doesn't match their definition of righteousness, justice, or compassion. The critique is often correct, of course, but the solution reflects Americans' typical impatience—a cultural trait often noticed by the global church. We must develop the virtue of patience.

To be clear, I'm not advocating for patience with sin but am begging for godly patience with sinners as God continues to sanctify. When we're tempted to distance ourselves from fellow American evangelicals for their lack of cultural captivity, let us consider Dietrich Bonhoeffer's words. Facing German Christian complicity with the Nazi regime, he wrote to his seminary community,

> One who wants more than what Christ has established does not want Christian brotherhood. He is looking for some extraordinary social experience which he has not found elsewhere; he is bringing muddled and impure desires into Christian brotherhood. . . . He who loves his dream of a community more than the Christian community itself becomes a destroyer of the latter, even though his personal intentions may be ever so honest and earnest

and sacrificial. If we do not give thanks daily for the Christian fellowship in which we have been placed, even where there is not great experience, no discoverable riches, but much weakness, small faith, and difficulty; if on the contrary, we only keep complaining to God that everything is so paltry and petty, so far from what we expected, then we hinder God from letting our fellowship grow according to the measure and riches which are there for us all in Jesus Christ.[15]

While confronting the reality of widespread moral compromise, Bonhoeffer continued to believe that God would complete the good work he had begun in German Christians. This made him patient, which, as the ultimate precursor to love, is a necessary precursor to change.

Activism. American evangelicals are often better known for the movements and networks they start than the institutions they sustain. This reflects a highly American, entrepreneurial, pragmatic goal orientation with a tendency to build ministries around visionary individuals. We take seriously the Great Commission and the Great Commandment, and so we focus our attention on fulfilling those two mandates. We constantly birth new ministries, new alliances, and new denominations that engage new generations, new cultures, and new situations.

Such activism provides another key to the renewal of evangelicalism. It offers unparalleled flexibility as a faith tradition and allows us to create new systems that address our current realities. Recent years have seen growing numbers of ministries engaging in historic areas of failure among evangelicals, such as racial justice, community development, human trafficking, and creation care. If we've failed to address issues in the past, we are much more open to addressing them now. *Semper reformanda.*

At the same time, an aversion to institutions undermines our ability to seek renewal and revival. American evangelicalism is a loosely related set of movements, networks, and institutions, so it struggles with two issues in the quest for reform.

First, networks and movements have no institutional responsibility because they are often short-lived (one or two generations). Addressing historic sins and culture failures requires the ability to engage consistently across time via institutions. For example, the descendants of 272 slaves sold to maintain the financial liquidity of Georgetown University in 1838 received apologies this year only because Georgetown University has existed for 228 years.[16]

Second, networks and movements, by nature, lack definitive authority structures. The lack of an authority structure, while providing great flexibility, also makes it exceedingly difficult to act consistently, speak collectively, or repent clearly. It can appear that no one is in charge. This makes it difficult for evangelicals to repent of sin or ask for forgiveness. (Who can speak for us?) Or promise a change of behavior. (Who can provide accountability?) As a result, we tend to communicate through social media, online petitions, and open letters—none of which lend themselves to nuanced conversations. It also leads to a particular kind of presentation by the media.

A colleague recently described the diversity of evangelicalism to the former president of one of the largest media networks in the America. He responded, "I had no idea that there were so many evangelicals who are as thoughtful and moderate as you. Why is that?" My friend pointed out that effective media storytelling requires two clearly opposing sides to delineate the issues. A moderate voice with nuance doesn't serve that purpose. In addition, evangelicalism's diffuse structure makes it difficult for one voice to be heard. Sadly, too often only the loudest and most extreme voices are noticed. Many of us shake our heads at the "evangelical leaders" that the news media anoints for us.

EVANGELICALISM IN THE NEXT GENERATION

The university campus seems like an unlikely source of hope for the future of evangelicalism. A recent study showed that faculty members are biased against evangelical faculty members. From anthropologists (59 percent) to English professors (53 percent), faculty shared that they would be less likely to hire someone they found out was an evangelical.[17] Traditional evangelical positions on human sexuality, abortion, and similar issues seem increasingly unwelcome. Younger people (including college students) are increasingly self-identifying as "nones"—people who have no religious belief.

Universities continue to state that nondiscrimination policies can prohibit religious groups from using faith-based criteria in selecting student leaders. Some, including Vanderbilt University, have suggested that even requiring a one-sentence affirmation of belief is discriminatory. Nevertheless, the university remains a place of hope as we consider evangelicalism's future. We see many Rock Chapels developing and thriving.

1. Record numbers of students are coming to faith in Christ. Over the past five years, InterVarsity has seen more students make first-time professions of faith than at any time in our seventy-five-year history. Partner ministries say the same thing.

This surprises many who have heard much about the rise of the nones[18] and the nearly even distribution between "religious," "spiritual," and "secular" on campus.[19] Our experience also suggests that the rapid erosion in the number of self-identified Christians doesn't necessarily reflect substantial defections from faith. Instead, it may represent the collapse of nominal cultural Christianity.[20] Most students no longer feel a need to identify as Christian.

This change represents a tremendous opportunity. It's easier to invite a self-identified non-Christian to come to faith than someone who is merely nominal. Strong conversions in college also may explain why evangelicals buck the trend experienced by most religious groups, which are experiencing a decline in the religious engagement of their students. According to a recent Pew Forum survey, 87 percent of evangelicals have high religious engagement, while that number is 54 percent for mainline Protestants and 62 percent for Catholics.[21]

2. There is a collaborative spirit in this generation to cross tribal, organizational, and historical boundaries. A few years ago, I was struck by an advertisement in a Chinese newspaper that had four corporate logos next to each other: UNICEF, Save the Children, Wycliffe Bible Translators, and IKEA. They were collaborating on a Chinese minority language project. UNICEF was invested because of the United Nations Millennium Development Goals, one of which is to develop minority languages as a key lever in combating poverty. Save the Children was a nonprofit beneficiary of this UNICEF initiative, as it would serve impoverished children. Wycliffe provided the boots on the ground and linguistic expertise. And IKEA was the corporate sponsor that funded the project. It encouraged me to think that the future of evangelicalism could include the regular collaboration of varying entities such as a nongovernmental organization, a for-profit furniture store, an evangelical organization, and a government entity.

This generation does collaboration in a new way—focused on mission, not on organization. It means divergent parts of the body of Christ—progressives and fundamentalists, denominations and networks—coming together in mission. It includes a willingness to collaborate even outside the body of Christ. This year in New England, an NCAA Division I athletic department is asking InterVarsity, an evangelical organization, to train its staff in crosscultural competency to help its athletic teams tackle racism. A large public California university is asking Inter-Varsity students to take over their international students' welcome week, developing programs to better orient them to American campus culture. An evangelical group at Washington University knocked on the door of the atheist Free Thinkers Society to invite it to collaborate on a community service project serving inner-city St. Louis. What was even more encouraging was that a few weeks later, the Free Thinkers Society knocked on the door at the evangelical group's meeting and asked whether they could do Bible studies together.

3. Evangelical campus ministries and churches are already taking steps to engage the future of evangelicalism: people of color. By 2040, white Americans will no longer be in the majority.[22] Ministries such as InterVarsity have already experienced this change and have adjusted ministry models accordingly. In 2016, 53 percent of InterVarsity's core students were students of color or international students. In this multiethnic environment, students are grappling with what Scripture says about ethnicity, race, justice, and grace. They find their attitudes and convictions changing. They are building crosscultural relationships. They are revising the narrative that assumes people with evangelical convictions are whites from the Midwest or South.

4. In the midst of fidelity to Christ's mission, we see fidelity to doctrine. In spite of universities challenging InterVarsity's access to campuses because of our faith-based requirement for leaders, no student group has abandoned its evangelical identity. Though opposition to our shared beliefs has been sharp, no group has chosen to change its doctrinal basis. These students have been castigated in the press, by administrators, and by fellow students. They have been drawn into yearlong administrative processes and court battles. In every single case, they have chosen to accept derecognition rather than surrender their evangelical identity and beliefs. One student leader said, "In recent years, it has been incredibly painful, difficult, and exhausting. But it has never been so clear to me—and to everyone in our fellowship—why our beliefs matter and why we need to clarify our identity."

For InterVarsity, this courage and clarity has been particularly gratifying. It reflects our origins, which can be traced to a student meeting held in Trinity College at Cambridge University in the summer of 1919. Norman Grubb and R. P. Dick, two leaders of the Cambridge InterCollegiate Christian Union (CICCU), met with ten leaders from the Student Christian Movement (SCM). Solidly evangelical, CICCU had been roundly derided for its faith, while SCM had drifted toward theological liberalism in the years after World War I but remained popular among students and faculty. They invited CICCU to merge with them. Grubb tells the story:

After an hour's talk, we appeared to be getting nowhere, so I asked their president point blank—"Does the SCM put the atoning blood of Jesus as *central* in its beliefs?" He hesitated and then answered, "Well, we acknowledge it, but not necessarily as central." The CICCU president . . . and I then said that this really settled the matter for us in the CICCU.[23]

They parted company. Within a few months, recognizing the need for a distinct evangelical witness on every university campus in Great Britain, they called for the first intervarsity (that is, inter-university) conference in December. Within a decade, they sent Howard Guinness to Canada to start Inter-Varsity there. Ten years later, InterVarsity was established in the United States with the same vision and aim.

Nearly a hundred years later—on campuses across the United States and in Rock Chapels in Ethiopia—college students have picked up the torch carried by their forebears. They embrace orthodox Christian faith and define their identity in the midst of pressure and contempt. Because of them, I'm hopeful about the future of evangelicalism.

NOTES

INTRODUCTION: STILL EVANGELICAL?

[1]Frank Newport, "Five Key Findings on Religion in the US," Gallup, December 23, 2016, www.gallup.com/poll/200186/five-key-findings-religion.aspx.

1 WILL EVANGELICALISM SURRENDER?

[1]Michael Cromartie, ed., *No Longer Exiles: The Religious Right in American Politics* (Washington, DC: Ethics and Public Policy Center, 1993), 26.

[2]Randall Balmer, *Thy Kingdom Come: An Evangelical's Lament* (New York: Basic Books, 2006), 14.

[3]Cromartie, *No Longer Exiles*, 26.

[4]Carol Anderson, *Eyes Off the Prize: The United Nations and the African American Struggle for Human Rights, 1944–1955* (Cambridge, UK: Cambridge University Press, 2003), 4-6, 12-15, 124-31.

[5]Angie Drobnic Holan, "Joe Wilson of South Carolina Said Obama Lied, but He Didn't," Politifact, September 9, 2009, www.politifact.com/truth-o -meter/statements/2009/sep/09/joe-wilson/joe-wilson-south-carolina-said -obama-lied-he-didn't-.

[6]Paul Kane, "'Tea Party' Protesters Accused of Spitting on Lawmaker, Using Slurs," *Washington Post*, March 20, 2010, www.washingtonpost.com/wp-dyn /content/article/2010/03/20/AR2010032002556.html.

[7]Gregory A. Smith and Jessica Martinez, "How the Faithful Voted: A Preliminary 2016 Analysis," Pew Research Center, www.pewresearch.org/fact -tank/2016/11/09/how-the-faithful-voted-a-preliminary-2016-analysis.

[8]White House Office of the Press Secretary, "Executive Order Protecting the Nation from Foreign Terrorist Entry into the United States," www.white house.gov/the-press-office/2017/03/06/executive-order-protecting-nation -foreign-terroristentry-united-states.

9Tal Kopan, "Democrats, Advocates Question ICE Raids After Hundreds of Arrests," CNN Politics, February 14, 2017, www.cnn.com/2017/02/10/politics /democrats-question-ice-enforcement-raids/index.html.

10Ann Doss Helms, "Sanctuary Schools? CMS Seeks Protection from Immigrant Arrests," *Charlotte Observer*, www.charlotteobserver.com/news/local /education/article132311804.html.

11Eric Lichtblau, "Sessions Indicates Justice Department Will Stop Monitoring Troubled Police Agencies," *New York Times*, February 28, 2017, www .nytimes.com/2017/02/28/us/politics/jeff-sessions-crime.html?_r=2. A version of this article appeared in print on March 1, 2017, on A1 of the New York edition, with the headline "Justice Dept. May Back Off Police Audits."

12Eric Lichtblau, "Justice Department Keeps For-Profit Prisons, Scrapping an Obama Plan," *New York Times*, February 23, 2017, www.nytimes .com/2017/02/23/us/politics/justice-department-private-prisons.html.

13Alice Miranda Ollstein, "Republicans Were Wildly Successful at Suppressing Voters in 2016: Three GOP-Controlled States Demonstrate the Effectiveness of Disenfranchising the Opposition," ThinkProgress, November 15, 2016, www.thinkprogress.org/2016-a-case-study-in-voter-suppression-258b5f90 ddcd.

14Sophia Tesfaye, "Jeff Sessions Drops DOJ Lawsuit Against Discriminatory Texas Voter ID Case, Reverses 6 Years of Litigation," Salon.com, February 27, 2017, www.salon.com/2017/02/27/jeff-sessions-drops-doj-lawsuit-against -discriminatory-texas-voter-id-case-reversing-6-years-of-litigation/.

15Gregory A. Smith, "Among White Evangelicals, Regular Churchgoers Are the Most Supportive of Trump," Pew Research Center, April 26, 2017, www.pewresearch.org/fact-tank/2017/04/26/among-white-evangelicals -regular-churchgoers-are-the-most-supportive-of-trump/.

2 WHY I AM AN EVANGELICAL

1D. W. Bebbington, *Evangelicalism in Modern Britain: A History from the 1730s to the 1980s* (London: Unwin Hyman, 1989), 5-17.

2Thomas Kidd, "'More a Doctrine Than a Person': Evangelicals and the Holy Spirit," Patheos, December 2, 2014, www.patheos.com/blogs/anxiousbench /2014/12/more-a-doctrine-than-a-person-evangelicals-and-the-holy-spirit/.

3This fascinating and well-documented history is compellingly described in Herbert Schlossberg's *The Silent Revolution and the Making of Victorian England* (Columbus: Ohio State University Press, 2000).

[4]John Wesley, "The Nature of Enthusiasm," Wesley Center Online, accessed August 25, 2017, wesley.nnu.edu/john-wesley/the-sermons-of-john-wesley -1872-edition/sermon-37-the-nature-of-enthusiasm/.

[5]See Karen Swallow Prior, "Hannah More and the Evangelical Influence on the English Novel," Liberty University dissertation, 1999, http://digital commons.liberty.edu/fac_dis/81/.

[6]Jonathan Edwards, "The True Christian's Life a Journey Towards Heaven," in *The Works of President Edwards* (New York: Leavitt & Allen, 1852), 4:575.

[7]As laid out by Mark Noll in *The Scandal of the Evangelical Mind* (Grand Rapids: Eerdmans, 1995).

[8]*The Works of the Reverend John Wesley* (New York: J. Emory and B. Waugh, 1831), 292.

[9]Samuel Richardson, *Pamela; or, Virtue Rewarded* (Oxford: Oxford University Press, 2001), 58.

[10]John Wolffe, *The Expansion of Evangelicalism: The Age of Wilberforce, More, Chalmers and Finney* (Downers Grove, IL: InterVarsity Press, 2007), 145-46.

3 RECAPTURING EVANGELICAL
IDENTITY AND MISSION

[1]I write as a white male born and raised in Appalachia. Therefore, my social location and personal history limit my understanding of the history and dynamics of evangelicalism in African American, Latino, and Asian communities. Furthermore, I write as one who has lived outside the United States and worked extensively with evangelicals on every continent. Although my perspective is international and missional, the focus of this chapter is on evangelicalism in the United States.

[2]Timothy George called 1976 "the year evangelicals came out of the prayer closet" in "Evangelicals and Others," *First Things*, February 2006, accessed April 7, 2017, www.firstthings.com/article/2006/02/evangelicals-and-others.

[3]See Pew Research Center, "Support for Same-Sex Marriage Grows, Even Among Groups That Had Been Skeptical," June 26, 2017, www.people -press.org/2017/06/26/support-for-same-sex-marriage-grows-even-among -groups-that-had-been-skeptical/. See also J. Daugherty and C. Copen, "Trends in Attitudes About Marriage, Childbearing, and Sexual Behavior: United States 2002, 2006–2010, and 2011–2013," *National Health Statistics Report*, no. 92, March 17, 2016; and Frank Newport, "Americans Continue

to Shift Left on Key Moral Issues," Gallup, May 26, 2015, www.gallup.com /poll/183413/americans-continue-shift-left-key-moral-issues.aspx.

[4]In "Rejecting the Religious Right," Holmes & Company, November 11, 2012, blogs.wickedlocal.com/holmesandco/2012/11/rejecting-the-reli gious-right/#axzz4LxPfgl5v. Cited in Frances FitzGerald, *The Evangelicals: The Struggle to Shape America* (New York: Simon & Schuster, 2017), 610.

[5]See Albert Mohler, "Character in Leadership—Does It Still Matter?," June 24, 2016, www.albertmohler.com/2016/06/24/character-leadership-still -matter/, and Jonathan Chate, "Religious Right Now Judgment-Free, Thanks to Donald Trump," *New York*, October 19, 2016, http://nymag.com /daily/intelligencer/2016/10/religious-right-now-judgment-free-thanks-to -donald-trump.html.

[6]Emma Green, "The Evangelical Reckoning over Donald Trump," *The Atlantic*, November 10, 2016, www.theatlantic.com/politics/archive/2016/11 /the-evangelical-reckoning-on-trump/507161/.

[7]David Bebbington, *Evangelicalism in Modern Britain: A History from the 1730s to the 1980s* (Abingdon, UK: Routledge, 1988).

[8]National Association of Evangelicals, "What Is an Evangelical?," accessed August 25, 2017, www.nae.net/what-is-an-evangelical/.

[9]Millard Erickson, *Christian Theology* (Grand Rapids: Baker Books, 1998), 1026.

[10]Bruce Hindmarsh, "Is Evangelical Ecclesiology an Oxymoron?," in *Evangelical Ecclesiology: Reality or Illusion?*, ed. John G. Stackhouse Jr. (Grand Rapids: Baker Academic, 2003), 15.

[11]George M. Marsden, *Understanding Fundamentalism and Evangelicalism* (Grand Rapids: Eerdmans, 1991), 2.

[12]See FitzGerald, *Evangelicals*

[13]See Randall Balmer's *Evangelicalism in America* (Waco, TX: Baylor University Press, 2016), Marsden's *Understanding Fundamentalism and Evangelicalism*, and Mark Noll's *The Rise of Evangelicalism: The Age of Edwards, Whitefield and the Wesleys* (Downers Grove, IL: IVP Academic, 2010) and *America's God: From Jonathan Edwards to Abraham Lincoln* (Oxford: Oxford University Press, 2002).

[14]See George Marsden's *Reforming Fundamentalism: Fuller Seminary and New Evangelicalism* (Grand Rapids: Eerdmans, 1987) and Grant Wacker's *America's Pastor: Billy Graham and the Shaping of a Nation* (Grand Rapids, Eerdmans, 1998).

[15]See Molly Worthen's *Apostles of Reason: The Crisis of Authority in American Evangelicalism* (Oxford: Oxford University Press, 2014).

[16]Scott Wenig, "A Man for All Evangelicals," *Christianity Today*, November 17, 2010, www.christianitytoday.com/ct/2010/november/24.50.html.

[17]FitzGerald, *Evangelicals*, 233.

[18]See Lesslie Newbigin, *The Household of God: Lectures on the Nature of the Church* (London: SCM Press, 1953); Darrel Guder, *The Continuing Conversion of the Church* (Grand Rapids: Eerdmans, 2000); Christopher J. H. Wright, *The Mission of God's People: A Biblical Theology of the Church's Mission* (Grand Rapids: Zondervan, 2010); Craig Van Gelder, ed., *The Missional Church in Context: Helping Congregations Develop Contextual Ministry* (Grand Rapids: Eerdmans, 2007).

[19]See Darrell Guder, *Missional Church: A Vision for the Sending of the Church in North America*, The Gospel and Our Culture Series (Grand Rapids: Eerdmans, 1998); Michael Goheen, *A Light to the Nations: The Missional Church and the Biblical Story* (Grand Rapids: Baker Academic, 2011), and Chris Wright, *The Mission of God: Unlocking the Bible's Grand Narrative* (Downers Grove, IL: InterVarsity Press, 2006).

[20]Mark Lau Branson, "Ecclesiology and Leadership for the Missional Church," in Van Gelder, *Missional Church in Context*, 94.

4 IMMIGRATION AND THE LATINA/O COMMUNITY

[1]Maria Sacchetti, "ICE immigration arrests of noncriminals double under Trump," *Washington Post*, April 16, 2017, www.washingtonpost.com/local/immigration-arrests-of-noncriminals-double-under-trump/2017/04/16/98a2f1e2-2096-11e7-be2a-3a1fb24d4671_story.html.

[2]Chris Sommerfeldt, Erin Kurkin, and Nancy Dillon, "Undocumented Woman with Brain Tumor Seized by Federal Agents at Texas Hospital, Family Fears She Will Die," *Daily News*, February 24, 2017, www.nydailynews.com/news/national/undocumented-woman-brain-tumor-removed-hospital-lawyer-article-1.2979956.

[3]Jade Hernandez, "Undocumented Dad Taken by ICE While Dropping Kids Off at School," *Eyewitness News*, March 3, 2017, http://abc7.com/news/undocumented-dad-taken-by-ice-while-dropping-kids-off-at-school/1782230/.

[4]Jonathan Blitzer, "The Woman Arrested by ICE in a Courthouse Speaks Out," *The New Yorker*, February 23, 2017, www.newyorker.com/news/news-desk/the-woman-arrested-by-ice-in-a-courthouse-speaks-out.

[5]Leo R. Chávez, *The Latino Threat: Constructing Immigrants, Citizens, and the Nation* (Stanford: Stanford University Press, 2008), 3.

[6]Zaragosa Vargas, *Crucible of Struggle: A History of Mexican Americans from the Colonial Period to the Present Era* (Oxford: Oxford University Press, 2010), 220.

[7]David Gutierrez, *Walls and Mirrors: Mexican Americans, Mexican Immigrants, and the Politics of Ethnicity* (Berkeley, CA: University of California Press, 1995), 142.

[8]Ian Gordon and Tasneem Raja, "164 Anti-Immigration Laws Passed Since 2010. A MoJo Analysis," *Mother Jones*, March/April 2012, www.motherjones .com/politics/2012/03/anti-immigration-law-database.

[9]Will Heilpern, "Trump Campaign: 11 Outrageous Quotes," CNN Politics, February 23, 2016, www.cnn.com/2015/12/31/politics/gallery/donald-trump -campaign-quotes/; "30 of Donald Trump's Wildest Quotes," CBS News, www.cbsnews.com/pictures/wild-donald-trump-quotes.

[10]For a more extensive and academic examination of this topic, see Robert Chao Romero, "Migration as Grace," *International Journal of Urban Transformation* 1, no. 1 (October 2016): 11-30.

[11]Virgilio Elizondo, *Galilean Journey: The Mexican American Promise* (Ossining, NY: Orbis, 2005), 91.

[12]Edward Schumacher-Matos, "How Illegal Immigrants Are Helping Social Security," *Washington Post*, Op Ed, September 3, 2010, www.washingtonpost .com/wp-dyn/content/article/2010/09/02/AR2010090202673.html.

[13]Jessica Vaughn, "Proposal to Axe Green Cards for Unskilled Workers Considered," *Center for Immigration Studies*, last modified October 28, 2011, http://cis.org/vaughan/green-cards-for-unskilled-workers.

5 EVANGELICAL FUTURES

[1]Jennifer M. Ortman and Christine E. Guarneri, "United States Population Projections: 2000 to 2050," United States Census Bureaus, www.census .gov/content/dam/Census/library/working-papers/2009/demo/us-pop -proj-2000-2050/analytical-document09.pdf.

[2]R. Stephen Warner, "Religion and New (Post-1965) Immigrants: Some Principles Drawn from Field Research," *American Studies* 41, no. 2/3 (Summer/Fall 2000): 271. See also Warner, "Coming to America: Immigrants and the Faith They Bring," *Christian Century* 121, no. 3 (February 10, 2004): 20-23; and R. Stephen Warner and Judith G. Wittner, eds., *Gath-*

erings in Diaspora: Religious Communities and the New Immigration (Philadelphia: Temple University Press, 1998).

[3]Mark Chaves, *American Religion: Contemporary Trends* (Princeton, NJ: Princeton University Press, 2011), 28-32. See also Elaine Ecklund, *Korean American Evangelicals* (New York: Oxford University Press, 2011), and Ana Maria Diaz-Stevens and Anthony M. Stevens-Arroyo, *Recognizing the Latino Resurgence in US Religion* (Boulder, CO: Westview Press, 1997).

[4]Warner, "Coming to America," 20.

[5]See Soong-Chan Rah, *The Next Evangelicalism* (Downers Grove, IL: InterVarsity Press, 2009).

[6]See Soong-Chan Rah, *Prophetic Lament* (Downers Grove, IL: InterVarsity Press, 2015).

[7]John Wilsey, *American Exceptionalism and Civil Religion: Reassessing the History of an Idea* (Downers Grove, IL: IVP Academic, 2015), 15.

[8]See Soong-Chan Rah and Gary Vanderpol, *Return to Justice: Six Movements That Reignited Our Contemporary Evangelical Conscience* (Grand Rapids: Brazos, 2016).

[9]Paul G. Hiebert, *Anthropological Reflections on Missiological Issues* (Grand Rapids: Baker Books, 1994), 110-18.

[10]Claus Westermann, *Praise and Lament in the Psalms* (Atlanta: John Knox Press, 1981), 152.

[11]Soong-Chan Rah, *Prophetic Lament: A Call for Justice in Troubled Times* (Downers Grove, IL: InterVarsity Press, 2105), Kindle locs. 169-76.

[12]A. G. Miller, "The Rise of African-American Evangelicalism in American Culture," in *Perspectives on American Religion and Culture*, ed. Peter W. Williams (Malden, MA: Blackwell Publishers, 1999), 261.

[13]Rah, *Prophetic Lament*, Kindle locs. 1314-17.

[14]See Rah and Vanderpol, *Return to Justice*.

6 THEOLOGY AND ORTHOPRAXIS IN
GLOBAL EVANGELICALISM

[1]Allen Yeh et al., *Routes and Radishes and Other Things to Talk About at the Evangelical Crossroads* (Grand Rapids: Zondervan, 2010).

[2]David Bebbington, *Evangelicalism in Modern Britain: A History from the 1730s to the 1980s* (London: Unwin Hyman, 1989), 2-3.

[3]William Wilberforce, *A Letter on the Abolition of the Slave Trade, Addressed to the Freeholders and Other Inhabitants of Yorkshire* (London, 1807).

⁴Alicia Fedelina Chavez and Susan Diana Longerbeam, *Teaching Across Cultural Strengths: A Guide to Balancing Integrated and Individuated Cultural Frameworks in College Teaching* (Sterling, VA: Stylus, 2016), 78.

⁵See N. T. Wright's books, for example, *What Saint Paul Really Said* (1997) and *Justification: God's Plan and Paul's Vision* (2009).

⁶S. Steve Kang, "Salient Theoretical Frameworks for Forming Kingdom Citizens," in *A Many Colored Kingdom: Multicultural Dynamics for Spiritual Formation*, ed. Elizabeth Conde-Frazier, S. Steve Kang, and Gary A. Parrett (Grand Rapids: Baker Academic, 2004), 83.

⁷James Bryan Smith, *Rich Mullins: An Arrow Pointing to Heaven: A Devotional Biography* (Nashville: B&H, 2000), 42.

⁸Paul G. Hiebert, *Anthropological Reflections on Missiological Issues* (Grand Rapids: Baker, 1994), 107.

⁹David Kinnaman, *unChristian: What a New Generation Really Thinks About Christianity . . . and Why It Matters* (Grand Rapids: Baker, 2012), 5.

¹⁰Leith Anderson, "Immigration and Migration, Globalization, Urbanization, and Exploitation," keynote address at the Evangelical Missiological Society national conference in Atlanta, September 26, 2014.

¹¹"McCain or Obama?," *PRISM*, September/October 2008, 46, 48.

¹²Also called the non-Western world, the Majority World, or the Global South.

¹³Philip Jenkins, *The Next Christendom: The Coming of Global Christianity* (Oxford: Oxford University Press, 2008), 8.

¹⁴Mark A. Noll, *The New Shape of World Christianity: How American Experience Reflects Global Faith* (Downers Grove, IL: InterVarsity Press, 2009), 109.

¹⁵Its full name is *An Enquiry into the Obligations of Christians to Use Means for the Conversion of the Heathens in which the Religious State of the Different Nations of the World, the Success of Former Undertakings, and the Practicability of Further Undertakings, are Considered.*

¹⁶Brian Stanley, *The World Missionary Conference, Edinburgh 1910* (Grand Rapids: Eerdmans, 2009), 9.

¹⁷Mark A. Noll, *Turning Points: Decisive Moments in the History of Christianity* (Grand Rapids: Baker Books, 2001), 7. His turning points: (1) The Fall of Jerusalem (AD 70); (2) The Council of Nicaea (325); (3) The Council of Chalcedon (451); (4) Benedict's Rule (530); (5) The Coronation of Charlemagne (800); (6) The Great Schism (1054); (7) The Diet of Worms (1521); (8) The English Act of Supremacy (1534); (9) The Founding of the Jesuits (1540); (10) The Conversion of the Wesleys (1738);

(11) The French Revolution (1789); (12) The Edinburgh World Missionary Conference (1910).

[18]For the fuller story of why these Middle Eastern Christians' histories are excluded from our narratives as if they never existed, see Philip Jenkins, *The Lost History of Christianity: The Thousand-Year Golden Age of the Church in the Middle East, Africa, and Asia—and How It Died* (New York: HarperCollins, 2008).

[19]Andrew F. Walls, *The Missionary Movement in Christian History: Studies in the Transmission of Faith* (Maryknoll, NY: Orbis, 1996), 5.

[20]Henry Venn, "Instructions to Missionaries, December 5, 1851," in *Bibliography of Henry Venn's Printed Writings with Index,* ed. Wilbert R. Shenk (Scottdale, PA: Herald Press, 1975), 80:427.

[21]Paul G. Hiebert, *Anthropological Reflections on Missiological Issues* (Grand Rapids: Baker, 1994), 97.

[22]Tokunboh Adeyemo, ed., *Africa Bible Commentary* (Grand Rapids: Zondervan, 2010), copublished with Word Alive Publishers in Kenya.

[23]Brian Wintle, ed., *South Asia Bible Commentary* (Grand Rapids: Zondervan, 2015), copublished with Open Door Publications in India.

[24]Barry Corey, *Love Kindness: Discover the Power of a Forgotten Christian Virtue* (Carol Stream, IL: Tyndale, 2016), 9.

[25]Duane Elmer, *Cross-Cultural Connections: Stepping Out and Fitting In Around the World* (Downers Grove, IL: IVP Academic, 2002), 22.

7 REMAINING TO REFORM

[1]Avery Cardinal Dulles, *A History of Apologetics* (Eugene, OR: Wipf and Stock Publishers, 1999), 50.

8 LOOKING FOR UNITY IN ALL THE WRONG PLACES

[1]Joan Williams, *Working Class: Overcoming Class Cluelessness in America* (Boston: Harvard Business Press, 2017), Kindle loc. 164.

[2]Perry Miller, *The New England Mind: The Seventeenth Century* (New York: Macmillan, 1939), 4.

[3]Ibid., 5.

9 EVANGELICALISM MUST BE BORN AGAIN

Some of the content in this chapter is drawn from Shane Claiborne and Tony Campolo, *Red Letter Revolution* (Nashville: Thomas Nelson, 2012), and Tony

Campolo and Shane Claiborne, "The Evangelicalism of Old White Men Is Dead," *New York Times*, November 29, 2016.

[1]Jim Wallis, "Evangelicals Aren't Who You Think," *USA Today*, October 23, 2016, www.usatoday.com/story/opinion/2016/10/23/evangelicals-trump -white-conservatives-identity-theft-jim-wallis/92355326.

[2]Bob Smietana, "Latest Survey: Most Evangelicals Are Not Voting Trump," *Christianity Today*, October 14, 2016, www.christianitytoday.com/news/2016 /october/most-evangelicals-not-voting-trump-beliefs-identity-lifeway.html, and Reuters, "Gary Johnson and Jill Stein Take a Small Chunk of the Vote from Clinton and Trump," September 11, 2016, http://polling.reuters.com/#poll /TM651Y15_26/filters/LIKELY:1,D20:1/dates/20160901-2016 1014/type/week.

[3]Wallis, "Evangelicals Aren't Who You Think."

[4]"Jerry Falwell Jr. Calls Donald Trump the 'Dream President' for Evangelicals," *HuffPost*, April 30, 2017, www.huffingtonpost.com/entry/jerry -falwell-jr-dream-president-trump_us_5906950fe4b05c3976807a08.

[5]Andy Crouch, "Speak Truth to Trump," *Christianity Today*, October 10, 2016, www.christianitytoday.com/ct/2016/october-web-only/speak-truth -to-trump.html.

[6]Russell D. Moore, "Can the Religious Right Be Saved?," *First Things*, January 2017, www.firstthings.com/article/2017/01/can-the-religious-right-be-saved.

[7]Ibid.

[8]Ibid.

[9]Ibid.

[10]Frederick Douglass, *Narrative of the Life of Frederick Douglass, an American Slave* (Boston: Anti-Slavery Office, 1845), appendix.

10 THE IMPORTANCE OF LISTENING IN TODAY'S EVANGELICALISM

[1]John Stott, *The Contemporary Christian* (Downers Grove, IL: InterVarsity Press, 1992), 101.

11 HOPE FOR THE NEXT GENERATION

[1]For a measured (if frustrated) perspective, see an opinion piece written during the 2016 US presidential election by the president of the Southern Baptist Convention's Ethics and Religious Liberty Commission. Russell Moore, "Russell Moore: Why This Election Makes Me Hate the Word

'Evangelical,'" *Washington Post*, February 29, 2016, www.washingtonpost
.com/news/acts-of-faith/wp/2016/02/29/russell-moore-why-this-election
-makes-me-hate-the-word-evangelical. Moore continues to identify proudly
as an evangelical.

[2]Tokunbo Adeyemo, ed., *The African Bible Commentary*, 2nd ed. (Grand
Rapids: Zondervan, 2010).

[3]Brian Wintle, ed., *The South Asian Bible Commentary* (Grand Rapids:
Zondervan, 2015).

[4]See, for example, E. Randolph Richards and Brandon J. O'Brien, *Misreading
Scripture with Western Eyes* (Downers Grove, IL: InterVarsity Press, 2012).

[5]See, for example, Graham Hill, *GlobalChurch: Reshaping Our Conversations,
Renewing Our Mission, Revitalizing Our Churches* (Downers Grove, IL: Inter-
Varsity Press, 2015). Hill, an Australian, interviewed more than one hundred
Majority World evangelical leaders to learn what they could teach the Western
evangelical church about mission, ministry, and leadership.

[6]"Jan 02: World, Global Hot Spots," Operation World, www.operationworld
.org/jan02, accessed May 12, 2017. See also Rob Moll, "Missions Incredible,"
Christianity Today, March 1, 2006, www.christianitytoday.com/ct/2006
/march/16.28.html.

[7]Nikki A. Toyama-Szeto and Femi B. Adeleye, *Partnering with the Global
Church* (Downers Grove, IL: InterVarsity Press, 2012).

[8]See, for example, John Stott, *Christ in Conflict*, rev. ed. (Downers Grove, IL:
InterVarsity Press, 2013), 28.

[9]Mark A. Noll, *The Rise of Evangelicalism* (Downers Grove, IL: InterVarsity
Press, 2003), 50-75.

[10]David W. Bebbington, *Evangelicalism in Modern Britain: A History from the
1730s to the 1980s* (London: Unwin Hyman, 1989), 2-17.

[11]Stott, *Christ in Conflict*, 198-205.

[12]Harold Ockenga, excerpt from sermon preached at Park Street Church,
Boston, on December 8, 1957.

[13]A classic evangelical expression of this can be found in John R. W. Stott, *The
Cross of Christ*, twentieth anniversary ed. (Downers Grove, IL: InterVarsity
Press, 2006). A more popular-level book that attempts to explain both this
belief and how it's experienced by evangelicals is Rebecca Manley Pippert,
Hope Has Its Reasons (Downers Grove, IL: InterVarsity Press, 2001).

[14]See, for example, Mae Cannon et al., *Forgive Us: Confessions of a Compromised Faith* (Grand Rapids: Zondervan, 2014).

[15]Dietrich Bonhoeffer, *Life Together* (New York: Harper & Row, 1954), 26-27, 29.

[16]Shawn Sullivan, "Georgetown University, Jesuits Formally Apologize for Role in Slavery," *USA Today*, April 18, 2017, www.usatoday.com/story/news/nation -now/2017/04/18/georgetown-university-jesuits-slavery-apology /100607942.

[17]George Yancey, *Compromising Scholarship: Religious and Conservative Bias in American Higher Education* (Waco, TX: Baylor University Press, 2017). See also Nicholas Kristof, "A Confession of Liberal Intolerance," *New York Times*, May 7, 2016, www.nytimes.com/2016/05/08/opinion/sunday/a-con fession-of-liberal-intolerance.html?mcubz=0.

[18]Michael Lipka, "A Closer Look at America's Rapidly Growing Religious 'Nones,'" Pew Research Center, May 13, 2015, www.pewresearch.org/fact-tank /2015/05/13/a-closer-look-at-americas-rapidly-growing-religious-nones.

[19]"U.S. College Students Evenly Divided Between Religious, Secular and Spiritual, in New ARIS Study," September 25, 2013, Center for Inquiry, www.centerforinquiry.net/newsroom/u.s._college_students_evenly_divided _between_religious_secular_and_spiritua/.

[20]This seems to be supported by Ed Stetzer's analysis of the data as well: "Nominals to Nones: 3 Key Takeaways from Pew's Religious Landscape Survey," *Christianity Today*, May 12, 2105, www.christianitytoday.com /edstetzer/2015/may/nominals-to-nones-3-key-takeaways-from-pews-reli gious-lands.html.

[21]"In America, Does More Education Equal Less Religion?," Pew Research Center, April 26, 2017, www.pewforum.org/2017/04/26/in-america-does -more-education-equal-less-religion/.

[22]Evan Horowitz, "When Will Minorities Be the Majority?," *Boston Globe*, February 26, 2016, www.bostonglobe.com/news/politics/2016/02/26/when- will-minor ities-majority/9v5m1Jj8hdGcXvpXtbQT5I/story.html.

[23]Keith and Gladys Hunt, *For Christ and the University* (Downers Grove, IL: InterVarsity Press, 1991), 57, citing Douglas Johnson, *Contending for the Faith: A History of the Evangelical Movement in the Universities and Colleges* (Leicester, UK: Inter-Varsity Press, 1979), 216.

CONTRIBUTORS

Shane Claiborne is an author, activist, speaker, and self-proclaimed "recovering sinner." He writes and speaks about peacemaking, social justice, and Jesus, and is the author of numerous books, including *The Irresistible Revolution, Jesus for President*, and *Executing Grace*. He is the leader of The Simple Way in Philadelphia and cofounder of Red Letter Christians.

Jim Daly is president of Focus on the Family and host of its daily broadcast, heard by more than 6.3 million listeners a week. Under his leadership, the ministry has reinvigorated its traditional focus on helping couples build strong marriages and raise healthy, resilient kids.

Mark Galli is editor in chief of *Christianity Today* and the author of *Karl Barth: An Introductory Biography for Evangelicals*.

Lisa Sharon Harper is a prolific speaker, writer, trainer, and activist, and founder and principal of FreedomRoad.us. She is the author of several books, including *The Very Good Gospel: How Everything Wrong Can Be Made Right*.

Tom Lin is president of InterVarsity Christian Fellowship and previously served as director of the Urbana Student Missions Conference. A trustee on the boards of Fuller Theological Seminary, Crowell Trust, and the Lausanne Movement, Tom holds degrees from Harvard University and Fuller Theological Seminary.

Karen Swallow Prior is an award-winning professor of English at Liberty University. She is the author of *Booked: Literature in the Soul of Me* and *Fierce Convictions: The Extraordinary Life of Hannah More—Poet, Reformer, Abolitionist*. She is a research fellow with the Ethics and Religious Liberty Commission of the Southern Baptist Convention.

Soong-Chan Rah is Milton B. Engebretson Professor of Church Growth and Evangelism at North Park Theological Seminary in Chicago. He is also the author of *The Next Evangelicalism*, *Many Colors*, and *Prophetic Lament*, and the coauthor of *Forgive Us* and *Return to Justice*. He holds a ThD from Duke University and a DMin from Gordon-Conwell Theological Seminary.

Robert Chao Romero is an associate professor in the Cesar E. Chavez Department of Chicana and Chicano Studies at the University of California, Los Angeles. He received his PhD in history from UCLA and his JD from UC Berkeley. He is the author of *The Chinese in Mexico* and *Jesus for Revolutionaries*.

Sandra Maria Van Opstal is the executive pastor of Grace and Peace Community on Chicago's West Side. She is a liturgist and activist who seeks to reimagine worship that mobilizes communities to reconciliation and justice. She is the author of *The Next Worship: Glorifying God in a Diverse World*.

Allen Yeh is associate professor of intercultural studies and missiology at Biola University, Cook School of Intercultural Studies. He also serves on the board of trustees of Foundation for Theological Education in Southeast Asia, was co-program chair of the 2017 Evangelical Missiological Society on Majority World Theology, and is the author of *Polycentric Missiology: Twenty-First Century Mission from Everyone to Everywhere*.

Mark Young is the president of Denver Seminary. Before coming to the seminary, he served as a missionary educator, a professor of world missions and intercultural studies, and a pastor. He remains actively engaged in global theological education.